Who Killed Canadian History?

Who Killed Canadian History?

J. L. GRANATSTEIN

HARPER **PERENNIAL**
A Phyllis Bruce Book

For David Bercuson,
comrade-in-arms

First published in hardcover by HarperCollins: 1998
First HarperPerennial edition: 1999
This revised edition: 2007

HARPER **PERENNIAL**
is a registered trademark of HarperCollins Publishers.

www.harpercollins.ca

Library and Archives Canada Cataloguing in Publication

Granatstein, J. L., 1939–
Who killed Canadian history? / J.L. Granatstein.

"A Phyllis Bruce book".
ISBN-13: 978-0-00-200895-2   ISBN-10: 0-00-200895-5

1. Canada—History—Study and teaching—Government policy.
2. Multiculturalism—Canada. 3. Education and state—Canada. I. Title.

LA417.5.G68 2007   379.71   C2007-903547-7

10 9 8 7 6 5 4 3

Contents

Acknowledgments VII

Preface to the Revised and Expanded Edition IX

Chapter 1 What History? Which History? 1

Chapter 2 Teaching Ignorance: History in the Schools 19

Chapter 3 Professing Trivia: The Academic Historians 53

Chapter 4 Multicultural Mania 83

Chapter 5 No Flanders Fields? Canadians, War,

  and Remembrance 117

Chapter 6 Hitler's Car and the State of Canadian History . . 141

Chapter 7 Canadian Identity and Canadian History 155

Chapter 8 Resurrecting Canadian History 171

Index 187

Acknowledgments

I am most grateful to Milena Ivkovic for splendid research assistance. I have also been assisted by a number of teachers who took the time to talk to me, by former university colleagues, and by friends William Kaplan, Bill Young, Graham Rawlinson, and Catherine Salo. Bill Blaikie, MP, obtained the Manitoba legislature debates on the teaching of Canadian history for me. Rudyard Griffiths and the Dominion Institute provided useful information and polling data on Canadians' historical knowledge, and Historica president Colin Robertson gave me access to studies done for that organization. I am grateful to them all.

J.L.G.

July 2007

Preface to the Revised and Expanded Edition

Whose history would we teach? That is the usual response from education ministers and school board officials to questions concerning why so little history is taught in our schools. It suggests that for a linguistically and geographically divided nation, for a country populated by immigrants, there are many histories—far too many for us to teach. Better to offer none at all or to subsume history in social studies and civic education.

The answer should be that we will teach the history of Canada, of all its people, of their role in developing this nation, and of Canada's place in the world. Somehow, unfortunately, that all-too-reasonable response never stirs to action those who shape provincial education policies. Yet the question "Whose history are we actually teaching?" is answered every day in our classrooms in ways that might surprise parents and taxpayers.

Ten years ago, Brad was a bright eight-year-old, a reader and a talker. George and Suzanne, his parents and my friends, paid $8,000 a year to send him to a small private school near their home in the Maritimes because, they were convinced, the school offered good teaching and high-quality learning. In Brad's "enhanced" grade 2 class that school year, he began to be taught something about his country, and he learned about Canadian geography, Quebec sugar bushes, and the Group of Seven. He also wrote five brief historical reports. The first report was on Samuel de Champlain, with substantial emphasis on the tribulations Champlain inflicted on his child-bride. The second examined the extinction of the Beothuk, thanks to shootings, disease, and starvation caused by the white men. The third was about Louis Riel, whom Brad called a Métis hero but who was labelled a traitor in his day because he stood up for his people. The next report outlined the opposition and frustration endured by Canada's first female doctor, Emily Jennings Stowe, as she sought to practise medicine in the face of the patriarchal medical establishment. The last, on the maltreatment of Japanese Canadians during the Second World War, dealt with what happened to people when, as Brad wrote, the government decided it could not trust anyone who looked Japanese.

Brad's papers were impressively written for an eight-year-old child, but profoundly depressing in what they suggested went on in our schools—and still does. To begin with, in most public schools in grade 2, no history at all would have been taught and no essay writing demanded. Brad was receiving advanced learning in his private school, exactly what his parents wanted and were paying to receive.

What they had not counted on was that the first exposure to the history of Canada that Brad received in class combined seemingly unrelated events and individuals—without much regard for chronology—that were judged important by his teacher. Though provincial guidelines offer little direction for early primary grades, the teacher was reflecting what she deemed to be the province's educational priorities. The material taught stressed the existence of anti-Aboriginal, anti-Métis, and anti-Asian racism, as well as male sexism and discrimination against women, as if these issues were and always had been the primary identifying characteristics of Canada. Riel, the first "hero" to whom Brad was exposed, in a country that always bewails its lack of them, was a man who, after a kangaroo-court trial, ordered the murder of a loud-mouthed Ontario Orangeman and, to boot, was a crazed religious fanatic who led two armed rebellions. Riel might be a hero and a leader to the Métis, but he has no credentials as a hero to all Canadians, and no school should teach his life that way.

Indeed, since all education is about choices, we might ask why Brad should learn about Riel rather than Sir John A. Macdonald, someone whose accomplishments were more important and much longer lasting. Or about Emily Stowe rather than Frederick Banting, the discoverer of insulin. Or about the maltreatment of Japanese Canadians rather than the successful integration of millions of immigrants.

The reasons, unfortunately, are all too obvious, and they provide the real answer to the question "Whose history should we teach?"

The choices being made every day in Brad's school and thousands of others are political, not historical. They aim to teach lessons about racism and sexism, not history. The history taught is that of the grievers among us, the present-day crusaders against public policy or discrimination. The history omitted is that of the Canadian nation and people.

There was racism and sexism in Canada's past, of course, just as there is today. We need to study these subjects, but these are not the only themes in our history, even if one would be hard-pressed to prove it from the history education offered to Canada's young schoolchildren. Sadly, Brad's experience is echoed in classrooms from Newfoundland to British Columbia. What are we saying to our sons and daughters and to those children who are new arrivals in our society? What are we doing to our history? Somewhere, somehow, we have completely lost our way.

Canada must be one of the few nations in the world, certainly one of the few Western industrialized states, that does not make an effort to teach its history positively and thoroughly to its young people. It must be one of the few political entities to overlook its own cultural traditions—the European civilization on which our nation is founded—on the grounds that to do otherwise would systematically discriminate against those who come from other cultures. The effects of these policies on a generation of students are all around us as the twenty-first century opens up before us.

History is important, I believe, because it is the way a nation, a people, and an individual learn who they are, where they came from and where they are going, and how and why their world has turned out as it has. We do not simply exist in a contemporary world, our eyes fixed to the TV or computer screen, our senses bombarded by transient images and sounds. We have a past, if only we would try to grapple with it.

History teaches us a sense of change over time. History is memory, inspiration, and commonality—and a nation without memory is every bit as adrift as an amnesiac wandering the streets. History matters, and we forget this truth at our peril.

It has now been almost a decade since the first edition of this book appeared. It has been quoted in Parliament and in provincial legislatures, and reviewed more extensively than anything else I have written. It has generated, and still generates, hundreds of letters to me from teachers, parents, and grandparents, alarmed at what is going on—or not going on—in our schools. The title has become a long-lasting catchphrase, one that can be dropped into unrelated articles or everyday speech without any necessity to explain its origin.

If only the message had been accepted. Some provincial governments made adjustments to their curricula, but most did nothing. With some wonderful exceptions scattered in classrooms across the country, most teachers have continued to teach what they always did in exactly the same ways. In Alberta, however, the Edmonton public schools joined forces with the University of Alberta History Department to redesign the history curriculum for grades 7, 8, and

9, and expanded its reach into grades 10 and 11. The Edmonton schools have also created a two-course series "The Military History of Canada" that, while aimed at one secondary school, the Vimy Ridge Academy, has received some interest from other high schools. There has been real progress among the vast majority who remain stuck in the mud.

At the same time, the private sector became interested anew in our history. Red Wilson, who in 1999 was chair of the powerful telecommunications firm BCE, read the first edition of *Who Killed Canadian History?* and called for the creation of a foundation for the history of Canada, offering $500,000 of his own funds to get it started. He attracted substantial interest from his business peers, and the result was Historica. The federal government spent large sums creating websites and portals that make accessing Canada's past easier for the computer literate. And the Canadian Broadcasting Corporation spent millions to produce a lavish multi-hour television "people's" history of Canada. What emerged from these ventures was not always top of the line, but the activity was all but unprecedented—and heartening.

I myself watched this growing interest in our past at the Canadian War Museum in Ottawa, where I was the director and CEO from July 1, 1998, to June 30, 2000. The War Museum had long been the orphan child of the Canadian national museum system. Underfunded, its exhibits static, its buildings completely inadequate, the museum had watched its attendance dwindle, and many harboured the secret fear that the government was simply waiting for the last veterans to disappear so that a museum that celebrated outdated virtues could be closed down.

It was not because the CWM lacked extraordinary material that it seemed irrelevant. First, it holds the wonderful official war art collection, of works created during the First and Second World Wars, the Korean War, and a succession of peacekeeping operations, peacemaking missions, and coalition wars. In all, the CWM has 13,000 pieces of art, with large samplings of work by the best Canadian artists, including members of the Group of Seven (to see Franz Johnston's superb paintings of Great War flying training, for example, is to stand in awe), Alex Colville, Paraskeva Clark, and Molly Lamb Bobak. The CWM has one of the world's great collections of military vehicles and a huge uniform collection, including the coatee General Brock was wearing when he was killed in action during the War of 1812. It holds a huge array of Canadian-won Victoria Crosses, a massive small-arms collection, the best military history library in Canada, and an archives with upwards of 500 manuscript collections. Unfortunately, it charged researchers to use the archival materials, almost alone among repositories in Canada, and CWM's prices for reproductions of photographs from its very good collection were double those charged by Library and Archives Canada. One of my first acts on going to the museum was to have a study done of these pricing policies and to eliminate the archival fee and reduce the reproduction costs.

For years, no one knew of the War Museum's superb collections. The art was scarcely ever seen—conditions in the War Museum on

Sussex Drive in Ottawa—the former Public Archives of Canada building, built early in the twentieth century—were so inadequate that artworks on paper could be displayed only for limited periods. The museum premises were so small that only 1 percent of the collection could be shown, and the warehouse—a former Ottawa streetcar barn—was far from ideal as a repository or a venue for visitors. Moreover, the archives were almost unusable because the funds to organize it so that researchers could plumb its treasures were never available.

But matters soon changed. Part of the change was caused by the first edition of this book, I think, but most was driven by the CBC's coverage of the fiftieth anniversaries of D-Day and V-E Day in 1994 and 1995, which attracted very large audiences at home and stirred interest in the men and women who had fought the Second World War. Attendance at Remembrance Day ceremonies began to rise as well.

That things were different soon was clear at the War Museum. The Donner Canadian Foundation made a very large grant to the museum to send around the country a travelling exhibit of the best war art and to produce a coffee-table book on the collection. Canvas of War, a superb exhibit, let Canadians see some of their hidden treasures. The archives were sorted and catalogued. And best of all, the government of Canada, in November 1998, gave the War Museum some eight hectares of land on the soon-to-be-disposed-of Canadian Forces Base Rockcliffe as the site for a new purpose-built museum. By 2000, the government had changed the location to Ottawa's LeBreton Flats and had put up the funding for a new Canadian War Museum, eventually $134 million in all. The new building and new exhibits, superb in every respect, opened to the public on V-E Day 2005, the sixtieth anniversary of the end of the Second World War. All this had been urged along by a media which had become focused on the need to recognize Canada's military past in an appropriate way. None of this would have happened twenty or thirty years ago. I believe that over time the existence of this historical museum, along with the Internet outreach it employs, will change the way Canada's past is understood and taught.

I claim no credit for this. It is clear that both the pressures to fix the War Museum and *Who Killed Canadian History?* simply caught waves that were already building across the country. Countless individuals helped this process along and deserve all the credit. What is important now is to ensure that the pressure to teach our history soundly and well is renewed, that parents demand that Canadian history be included in the elementary and high school curricula in every province, that schools stretch their existing curricula to the fullest to include Canada's past in their offerings, and that the media, business, and the federal government continue to assist in the process.

We do have a history. Canadians have an honourable past that merits study and that can unite us all, native-born and recent immigrants. We have a country to build.

Toronto

July 2007

CHAPTER 1

What History?
Which History?

Conservatives falsify the past, socialists falsify the future, and liberals falsify the present, so someone once said. It may even be true—in most countries. Canada is different.

Ours is a nation where everyone—liberal, socialist, and conservative—seems to be engaged in an unthinking conspiracy to eliminate Canada's past. The elementary and high schools scarcely teach history, so busy are they fighting racism, teaching sex education, or instructing English as a second language for recent immigrants. Fewer and fewer university professors write history in anything but undigestible small chunks of interest only to specialists. Most of the media use history only to search for villainy, if they use it at all, or else they mangle it beyond recognition to prove a contemporary argument. There are no heroes in our past to stir the soul, and no myths on which a national spirit can be built—or so we are told. The ordinary Canadian citizen, inundated by American media and Fourth of July rah-rah patriotism, scarcely knows that Canada has a past. Wasn't George Washington Canada's first prime minister? Didn't Davy Crockett settle the west?

Indeed, it sometimes seems that Canadians have deliberately deconstructed their past, sacrificing it for the good of a mythical present. The French Canadians were brave voyageurs who fought the Iroquois and the English, posing, in between, for Cornelius Krieghoff. The Loyalists were slaveholding Anglo-Saxon white males whose anti-democratic instincts were all too evident. Confederation was a scheme by railway investors to protect their profits. The Riel rebellions were attempts to thwart efforts to crush the idyllic civilizations of Native peoples under the weight of technology and speculators. If Canada participated in the two world wars, it should not have, because Canadians are peacekeepers by nature. This ignorant bowdlerization, where it has any intention at all, serves a nation that today sees itself as bilingual, multicultural, pacifist, and committed to social justice, peacekeeping, and medicare.

These are not evil national goals, to be sure, though they scarcely represent the Canada that most Canadians know. Even though each generation always writes its own history, the past is not supposed to be twisted completely out of shape to serve present ends. To do so mocks the dead and makes fools of the living; it reduces the past to a simplistic perspective on the present; and it imprisons history in a cage of consciously constructed quasi-fabrications. As Germans, Japanese, and Russians surely know, nations have to overcome their histories. Canada, thank heavens, has a relatively benign history, but, where we consider it at all, we struggle against the past as if our fore-bears had committed atrocities and innumerable evils, and regularly

4

practised genocidal behaviour. The task of the current generation is to build on the past, to understand it, and, where necessary, to triumph over it. If we cannot, the fault is not in what happened one, two, or three centuries ago, but in ourselves.

History is important because it helps people know themselves. It tells them who they were and who they are; it is the collective memory of humanity that situates them in their time and place; and it provides newcomers with some understanding of the society in which they have chosen to live. Of course, the collective memory undergoes constant revision, restructuring, and rewriting, but, whatever its form, it reveals anew to each generation a common fund of knowledge, traditions, values, and ideas that help to explain our existence and the mistakes and successes of the past.

Surely this process is all the more important in a world that is shrinking technologically and, simultaneously, fragmenting into ethnic and national groupings. Canada is part of a global economy and an integrated North American trading system, both of which bring stress to citizens and to governments. It is a nation of regions, languages, religions, and disparate classes and cultures. There is much to disunify Canadians and, all too often, very little to join them together. History is one such unifying factor: the way of life, the traditions, and the institutions that men and women created in this nation. For incomprehensible reasons, we have not passed this knowledge on to our children and to those who have recently arrived in Canada.

This neglect is foolhardy, for the past has shaped us all. Canada

5

was a French colony, then a British colony, and now, many might argue, an American one. This colonization has stunted Canadians' psychological development in important ways. Robert MacNeil, the Canadian-born newscaster who made PBS news a nightly event, wrote of his childhood, "One of the psychologically crippling things, part of the colonial wound that never healed at least in the psyches of my generation, was that we grew up reading books that were all written and published about people who lived . . . in other countries. We were not a written-about people. If you are not a written-about people, if you're not a storied people, you're not a people, you have no identity really." The fact is not that Canada has no past, but simply that its history has not been turned into story for Canadians. Much more Canadian history, and vastly more Canadian fiction, is written today than when MacNeil was a boy in Halifax, but it is as little understood by Canadians now as it was then.

Canadians have not tried to understand their past, so it should come as no surprise that they know little about it. Survey after survey has proven this ignorance beyond dispute. The Committee for an Independent Canada, in 1974, sponsored a Canadian history test in some British Columbia schools and found that three-quarters of the participants could not name the premier of Quebec or the capital of New Brunswick, six in ten were unable to name a single Canadian author, and large numbers did not know what the British North America Act was. The next year, publisher Mel Hurtig conducted a national test that produced

6

similar results. Two in three students could not name three prime ministers since the Second World War, or which Canadian won the Nobel Peace Prize in 1957. Lack of knowledge of geography, history, and literature was staggering, and 62 percent of the students taking the test failed abysmally.

In his memoirs, *At Twilight in the Country*, Hurtig detailed the extraordinary response to the publication of the results. Parliamentarians and provincial leaders were outraged, newspapers wrote editorials lamenting the situation, and individuals and groups demanded that school curricula in Canada be changed to correct the situation. Predictably, nothing happened.

The Task Force on National Unity, led by Keith Spicer at the beginning of the 1990s, heard from countless Canadians that they did not know their history and that they wanted more of it taught in school. Spicer concluded, "We do not know enough about ourselves. Without a radically fresh approach to improving what we know about each other, our lack of knowledge of the basic realities of this country will continue to cripple efforts at accommodation." Again, nothing resulted.

Then, in 1991, a national heritage test was conducted by the Association for Canadian Studies. Not surprisingly, the test again uncovered clear cultural gaps—English Canadians knew less Quebec history than Québécois did, and vice versa. The survey also found that Canadians, both French- and English-speaking, wanted more history and heritage taught in the schools and that they were concerned about how little they knew. Contrary to the popular myth, though, this was not because Canadian history was boring. Teach more history, the message went, and this common understanding might help tie Canadians together. Once more, no action resulted.

When Joanne Harris Burgess, a Canadian Studies professor at York University's Glendon College in Toronto, tested students in her course in 1997, she concluded, "I have noticed surprising, constantly growing gaps in my first-year students' knowledge of Canada." The results were startlingly similar to those Hurtig had found: two-thirds could not name a Canadian author; a large majority were unable to name the nation's first English- and French-speaking prime ministers; and more than half were unable to give the date of Confederation. "When the average mark of bright, interested Ontario high school graduates on this questionnaire is 32.5 percent," Professor Burgess wrote, "it is not the students but Canadian history courses in our high schools that have failed. And that is a failure we as a nation cannot afford."*

Similarly depressing results were found in a survey of young French- and English-speaking Canadians between the ages of eighteen and twenty-four conducted in late May 1997 by the Angus Reid Group for the then brand-new Dominion Institute. Just 54

8

---

* In the United States, testing sponsored by the National Centre for Education and conducted as part of the National Assessment of Education Programs in 2006 found an improvement—small but significant—in student knowledge of U.S. history in grades 4, 8, and 12 since 2001. Would Canadian results be the same? I doubt it, but, of course, Canada has no National Centre for Education and no National Assessment of Education Programs, so how would we ever know?

percent of respondents in the survey could identify John A. Macdonald as the nation's first prime minister, 33 percent were aware that Remembrance Day commemorated the end of the First World War, 35 percent knew what D-Day signified, 10 percent could define the Quiet Revolution, and a mere 14 percent could say why Lester Pearson had won the Nobel Peace Prize. Only 26 percent could name a war in which the United States invaded Canada (the Revolutionary War or the War of 1812), only 23 percent could identify the Loyalists, and 34 percent knew that the Acadians had been deported in the eighteenth century. The results were just as appalling on cultural questions. While 68 percent could pick Emily Carr as a Canadian artist, 30 percent thought Norman Rockwell was Canadian, as did 20 percent Allan Ginsberg, and 17 percent Tennessee Williams and Andy Warhol. Only 27 percent could identify Robert Service as Canadian, and a frighteningly low 11 percent knew that Sir Frederick Banting had won the Nobel Prize in medicine for his discovery of insulin. And it wasn't just ancient Canadian history that drew a blank: only 16 percent could identify Marc Garneau as the first Canadian in space. Overall, Canadian youth scored just 34 percent on this test. Forty percent of those questioned, the Angus Reid Group reported, drew the proper conclusion: They did not know as much as they should.

9

The results, said the Dominion Institute's director, Rudyard Griffiths, demonstrated all too clearly that Canadian youth have a very poor knowledge of the history of the relationship between French and English Canadians—and much else: "The survey indicates that we have failed to impart to our youth the histori-cal knowledge that is necessary to make informed decisions and sustain a sense of belonging." The Dominion Institute's subse-quent annual surveys have reinforced this conclusion with dreary predictability; indeed, the 2007 Canada Day survey showed a decline in knowledge compared to the 1997 results.

Canadian youth also have no Canadian reference points, few world reference points, and no basic knowledge. In his able book *In School: Our Kids, Our Teachers, Our Classrooms*, written before he became a politician, Ken Dryden noted one teacher's lament that the students in his Mississauga, Ontario, high school classroom didn't know the names of provinces, capital cities, or prime minis-ters. They recognized Bill Clinton's name more often than Jean Chrétien's because Clinton was more likely to be mentioned on the American television shows they watched. Most young people cannot place important global historical figures such as Winston Churchill or Franklin Roosevelt; Hitler is all but unknown, and Stalin and Mao Zedong are names they may have heard once or twice. Few are able to give the dates of the First or Second World War, or the combatants, or even which side Canada was on. And beyond this century, their ignorance is complete. They cannot describe, or give approximate dates for, Napoleon, the Renaissance, the Industrial Revolution, or the Norman Conquest. Nor are they any more knowledgeable about technology, literature, science, or geography, although all of them can handle computers with skill and connect to chat lines and put their data (and read others') on YouTube or

Facebook.* In effect, most students are culturally illiterate about everything beyond their generation's immediate experience.

What is the reason for this dangerous knowledge vacuum? To Dryden, it was the fact that today's students don't talk about current events around the dinner table the way his generation did. That may well be true, though it generalizes from one man's middle-class experience and neglects the explosion of media and the proliferation of computer games that absorb children and teenagers today. In any case, if the dinner-table conversations have disappeared, that is all the more reason for the schools to provide the cultural/political/historical reference points that every Canadian citizen requires.

The simple truth is that Canada's public and high schools have not only stopped teaching most world history, but have also given up teaching anything we might call Canadian or national history. As a result, Canadian students rarely learn anything of their country's past or its place in world history. There is nothing by way of national standards for history, and scarcely any prospect that such standards could be agreed upon. In contrast, there have been attempts to establish such standards in the United States and in Britain, usually in response to a perceived lack of historical knowledge on the part of young people. The situation in Canadian

11

---

* I acknowledge my debt here to E. D. Hirsch Jr., *Cultural Literacy* (New York 1988), which contains a sixty-page list of terms, dates, phrases, and quotations that "every American needs to know." The list is tilted heavily toward American references, but it is a good starting point for a definition of cultural literacy that adult Canadians could well read and contemplate.

universities is superficially better—certainly there are more Canadian historians employed and in training than at any time in our past. Still, survey courses increasingly reflect professorial interests, and those interests tend away from national and political history—the basic nuts and bolts of Canadian historical knowledge—toward such areas as gender, labour, and regional or local social history.

As a result, national history has increasingly been left to journalists to write or to private foundations to promote on television or in print. Pierre Berton, Peter C. Newman, and a few other popularizers have become the interpreters of our past for those who have the interest to read or the money to buy their books. Sometimes the journalists do this job well. Berton, for example, is probably responsible for much of the little interest there is in Canada's past. His books on the building of the Canadian Pacific Railway, Vimy, the Dionne quintuplets, and a host of other topics ranging from the Klondike to the story of Niagara Falls are exciting tales that have consciously tried to create Canadian myths and heroes. The historical minutiae are sacrificed for the telling incident, but that is understandable, even necessary. As Andrew Cohen noted, Berton and Newman are "the two great popularizers . . . of our history. We owe them a debt." (If only, he adds, sticking in the knife and twisting it, "the professional historians could bring the same passion to our past.") Nonetheless, popular national history in Canada, these notable exceptions aside, is in little better shape than is academic history.

The Charles R. Bronfman Foundation, and later Historica, tried to improve this situation by funding Heritage Minutes. Beautifully produced and historically accurate, these brief television vignettes bring some Canadian history to the usually vapid television fare. By turning history into melodrama, the CRB Foundation's teleplays have unquestionably helped to popularize history with some young people. The subjects covered in Heritage Minutes have become magnets drawing student essay writers, for example, and the series eventually may create a demand for a more systematic study of the past. This is all to the good, as are the historical comic books that the same foundation, in cooperation with McDonald's, distributed widely in the late 1990s. The first comic, on the Halifax Explosion, told Canadian children something they did not know before (though only 38 percent of them knew what the explosion was on the Dominion Institute quiz, given after the comic was distributed). Vignettes and comics, snippets and bowdlerized history, however, can only do so much, and no one should take them seriously as a substitute for the sustained study of the Canadian past.

Why have Canada's elementary and high schools failed to teach students about their national history? The Constitution gives control over education to the provinces, which guard their rights jealously. Quebec's quasi-federalist and separatist governments have had little interest in teaching anything but Quebec history, along with the litany of humiliations inflicted by federal governments and Anglo-Canadians that constitute the basis of Québécois grievances and nationalism. Maritime curricula, just like those in the Prairies and in British Columbia, have become ever more narrow, concentrating on the locality and the region rather than on the nation. The idea that there should be national standards in history seems to be a political non-starter. We need them, nonetheless.

It is not only the Constitution that is at fault. The ministries of education in our provincial capitals and the boards of education in our cities and towns have bought holus-bolus every trendy theory to emerge from university faculties of education. The progressive theories of education they espouse are child-centred rather than knowledge-based. The aim is to teach problem solving and critical thinking, not content. Facts are unimportant and can always be looked up on the Internet. Those who think that content is important are slavish practitioners of old-fashioned "rote learning." The result is a generation of students who are totally ignorant of anything not beamed into their brains via TV, movies, comic books, and the Internet.

Nor is it only the young who have been robbed of their past. Very few television programs are devoted to the history of Canada—though the advent of the History Television channel has greatly increased the quantity—and those that are produced are often biased in the extreme. Television programs on the internment of Italians suspected of Fascist sympathies or on the evacuation of Japanese Canadians from the west coast in 1942, for example, have painted brutal and bigoted wartime Canadians as the moral equivalents of those they fought in the Second World War. They were not, and only a nation robbed of its past could ever have allowed such tendentious material to air unchallenged. A CBC series such as *The Valour and the Horror*, which pretended to be a dramatized documentary about Canadian participation in the Second World War, created a furor, largely because it had no context. Only federal agencies fundamentally unaware of history could have funded such programming. Worse yet, the media rallied as one to defend the writer-producers, the McKenna brothers, against the protests from veterans and parliamentarians. Freedom of speech was one of the goals these veterans had fought to preserve, and few ever expected it to be used against their courageous efforts in such a way.

The veterans, at least, knew that their history was being taken away from them. What of the millions of immigrants who continue to pour into Canada? Coming from Hong Kong, Somalia, Russia, Israel, the Muslim world, and Central and South America, they end up in Vancouver, Winnipeg, Toronto, and a thousand small towns. They have chosen to become Canadians. But what does Canadian society say to them? Send your children to school to learn English or French, but, have no fear, nothing about the foundations of your new country will sully their ears or minds. That Canada seems to be a nation without a past, without roots, must surprise those who listen to what their children tell them about school. They soon discover that there is little to distinguish schoolyard or teenage culture in Canada from the American culture that dominates the television screen.

And the adults? If they choose to become citizens—and many do not—they are supposed to learn the contents of a pamphlet called *A Look at Canada*, published by Citizenship and Immigration Canada. It is a thorough test, with two hundred questions

15

on history, geography, and civics. Theoretically, if applicants for citizenship study the booklet, they will know many of the essential facts about Canada. Many diligently study the booklet; many appear to have realized that no one will question them on their knowledge of Canada. What government, eager for the ethnic vote, would dare to reject a Canadian citizenship applicant because he or she knew nothing of Canada? That would likely be grounds for a Charter challenge!

The cultural challenge facing new Canadians is more serious than passing a test. How do they integrate into this strange new society when the federal government (and at least one province, Quebec) has its own definition of assimilation? The federal government, committed to a multiculturalism that is enshrined in the Constitution as a fundamental characteristic of the nation, promotes a very weak nationalism. Remain a Somali, a Taiwanese, a Ukrainian, a Pakistani, or a Bolivian, the message goes, and you will be just as good a Canadian as everyone else. In effect, the message is that Canada (or English Canada, at least) has no culture. Moreover, the federal, provincial, and municipal governments will give any group money to preserve its original culture, heritage, and language. In Quebec, in sharp contrast, the provincial government controls immigration policy and follows what seems to be a deliberately anti-Canadian approach as it half-heartedly tries to assimilate immigrants into a francophone culture that sometimes seems to be less than warm to newcomers.

Ottawa's policy toward immigrants aims to encourage slow integration and to preserve the cultural mosaic in a nation that is marked by tolerance and goodwill. This approach may be well intentioned, but is it sound when no effort, other than the citizenship test, is made to teach newcomers that Canada is a democratic nation with a past, with traditions, with a history? No one should be surprised, therefore, that the Croatian defence minister in the mid-1990s was a Canadian who had returned "home" when the civil war erupted in Yugoslavia and who quickly began to engage himself in ethnic cleansing. No one should find it unusual that Serbian and Croatian Canadians, born in Canada, returned "home" to fight against the boys they went to high school with, and on some occasions against Canadian soldiers sent to keep the peace in their fratricidal new nations. (One Serb Canadian took a Canadian UN observer hostage and chained him to a pole in an area that seemed likely to be a target for NATO bombing. When the Serb returned to Canada, he was tried and found guilty for his crimes.) Unthinking Canadians complacently assumed that our schools and our society had turned immigrants all into good, bland, peace-loving Canadians. But a combination of federal multiculturalism, ignorance of the values of and lack of understanding of their new homeland, and the practices of progressive education had prevented immigrants from becoming what they ought to have become: Canadians.

17

As a historian, I believe that an understanding of our history is important in and of itself. But history has a public purpose, too, in creating Canadians who know where they want their nation to go in the coming years because they understand where the country has been. I believe that the achievements of the past, and even the failures of years gone by, can be a source of strength to meet not only today's challenges, but tomorrow's, too. If written and taught properly, history is not myth or chauvinism, just as national history is not perfervid nationalism; rather, history and nationalism are about understanding this country's past and how the past has made our present and is shaping our future. Moreover, I believe that the past can unite us without its being censored, made inoffensive to this group or that, or whitewashed to cover up the sins of our forefathers. If our history is to achieve this great national purpose, then major changes are needed in our schools and universities.

CHAPTER 2

Teaching Ignorance:
History in the Schools

"Historians," Soviet leader Nikita Khrushchev once said, "are dangerous people. They are capable of upsetting everything." The Russian leader understood that history matters because it is concerned with real people and with the way human lives have changed, for better or worse, over time. Small wonder it frightened Khrushchev.

The teaching of history is important because knowledge of the past is the prerequisite of political intelligence. Without history, the National Center for History in the Schools (University of California) has stated in its National Standards for World History, a society shares no common memory of where it has been, what its basic values are, or what past decisions have created its present circumstances. Without history, we as a nation cannot undertake any rational inquiry into the political, social, or moral issues of our society. And without historical knowledge and inquiry, we cannot achieve the informed citizenship that is essential for effective participation in the democratic process and in the fulfilment of all our democratic ideals. As the Report of Ontario's Royal Commission on Learning put it more than a decade ago, in 1995, students must have the opportunity to relate the past to the present: "Students, who will be voters, must understand . . . those links." To me, this is the key—the best of all reasons for making history a prominent part of the school curriculum.

How have Canadian schools handled this task of teaching the past to help prepare good, politically aware citizens? How have school boards and provincial governments done the job? Given the abysmal lack of basic knowledge of the Canadian past outlined in Chapter 1, the answer can only be "not very well." The general level of Canadian public debate and its contemporary focus, particularly around election times, are appalling. We have watched prime ministers pander to anti-Americanism, and we have observed premiers of Quebec—and of other provinces—flatly lie about constitutional questions. Other than a few columnists with large clipping files, who cares? Who remembers?

The lament for the state of Canadians' knowledge of their long-ago or immediate past is not new. George Ross, the Ontario minister of education in the 1880s, wanted Canadian history to be studied and "to reach more of Canada": "As Canadians," he said, "we should have a Canadian history, fearless in exalting the great actions of Canada's greatest men." The histories in use across the country were "merely provincial histories, without reference to our common country."

Nothing much changed over the next seventy years. Then in

1965, A.B. Hodgetts, a history teacher at Trinity College School in Port Hope, Ontario, persuaded his board of governors to fund a National History Project. It was an assessment of Canadian civic education, a study of the impact of the schools in developing the attitudes of young Canadians toward their country. Hodgetts believed that the study of Canada should be "one of the most vital subjects taught in our schools and . . . could become a much more effective instrument . . . in the fostering of understanding among [the Canadian] people." Completed in 1968 and published under the title *What Culture? What Heritage?*, the Hodgetts study pointed to stultifying teaching methods, the boredom of students, a dearth of good published work on Canada, and a glut of textbooks that offered bland consensus versions of the Canadian past. Canadian history was widely perceived as dull, and, as a discrete subject, it tended to disappear after the 1930s; after that point, high school courses became a mush of British, American, and European history.* Teachers seemed neither to know nor to care about Canadian topics, Hodgetts found, and most of them simply lectured from textbooks. As a result, Canadian students knew almost nothing of their own country. How then could they become good citizens?

Hodgetts's report sparked a growth in interest in Canada, something that fed on the nationalism unleashed by the centennial of Confederation, Expo 67, and the emergence of Pierre Trudeau, a

23

---

* The 1960 high school curriculum in Ontario, for example, included British history in grade 9, Canadian, U.S., and British history in grade 10, ancient and medieval history in grade 11, modern European history in grade 12, and Canadian and U.S. history in grade 13.

very different kind of Canadian leader. Soon the study of Canada seemed to be firmly ensconced in the schools and the universities. Provincial governments began to stress "Canadian studies," book-publishing programs received a boost, and the Secretary of State in Ottawa offered up generous funding to supplement the money available from foundations. Everything was for the best in the best of all possible worlds. Or was it?

The boom in Canadian studies turned out to be very different from an interest in the Canadian past. Canadian studies was not a single discipline with a methodological basis; instead, it was whatever those who taught something, anything, about Canada wanted it to be—an amalgam of literature, art, current events, politics and public issues, and the environment. There was very little room here for a systematic study of the past, let alone the Canadian past. Canadian studies was seen as relevant and therefore accessible and of interest to students; Canadian history was not. Administrators, pressed by their education ministries and school boards to keep the kids interested, began to hack and slash at history courses. It was, after all, an age in which the theories of interdisciplinary education espoused in *Living and Learning*—the Ontario Hall-Dennis Report of 1968—were changing the focus of the schools to a struggle to raise the self-esteem of students. The net effect of *What Culture? What Heritage?*, a book that initially had seemed to restore a new and enlivened history to the centre of the Canadian school curriculum, instead turned out to be a death knell. In Ontario, the nation's most populous province, history became the Latin of the 1970s and 1980s: history courses as a percentage of all high school courses went from 11.4 percent in 1964 to 6.6 percent in 1981–82. Today, Ontario requires only one compulsory history course in high school, and even that (on Canada since 1914) is too often as much current events and sociology-speak as history.

The Canadian-studies boom was part of a larger shift in attitudes toward learning. Developmental psychologists suggested that history was too complicated for young minds to grasp. History was so damned illogical, and it had nothing like the structure and coherence of, say, mathematics or science. At the same time, progressive educators argued that the role of schools was to foster the "development" of students, not to stuff them full of knowledge. It was all "child-centred" learning now, and testing fell into disfavour. Still others spoke about "behavioural objectives" or "accountability," and "relevance" and "self-realization" became sacred goals. In society at large (and especially after the Canadian Charter of Rights and Freedoms came into force in 1982), the emphasis shifted from community to individual rights and freedoms, and, outside Quebec, group rights began to be seen as antidemocratic. The schools reflected the shift. But almost no one called for history as a way of training the individual to be a good citizen, or of maintaining our heritage (except in the area of multicultural education), or of fostering an understanding of where this nation and its people had been and how they had developed. To educational theorists, history was boring, irrelevant, and fit

25

only for the slag heap, except for small nuggets that could be pulled out of the past and made useful for current concerns about racism, gender equity, and the plight of Native peoples. That all this trashing of history and heritage would be destructive and divisive, rather than a uniting force, did not seem to be noticed or, if it was, to matter.

While the new Canadian studies watered down the traditional approach to history and the progressive educators dismissed content-based learning, the provinces increasingly insisted on expanding their autonomy. Education is a provincial responsibility in Canada, and it always has been. By definition, this means there will be ten different ways of approaching the teaching of history in Canada, plus three more for the territories. Each province decides what history it will teach, when it will teach it, and what texts it will permit to be used. Obviously, the teaching of Canadian history in Quebec's French-language schools will be very different from that undertaken in Newfoundland or Saskatchewan; in fact, many provinces put their own history or that of their region first. As the federal government has no preordained role in education, it has tended not even to seek one for itself except at the university funding level and in minor ways as a facilitator. As a result, there are no measurable national standards for history (or any other subject) in Canada, no National Centre for History in the Schools, and slim prospects for the establishment of any of these things. Nor do we have a system of advanced placement courses that let the brightest high school

26

students do university-level work in certain subjects and get university credit for them.

We do not even have the equivalent of the *Studienstiftung des Deutschen Volkes*, a nationwide system of income-based scholarships that go to the very best German students selected in the high schools or, for late bloomers, the universities. For four decades, the winners of this national talent search have shown up in every sector of German public life and the universities as the meritocratic élite from which the nation draws its strength. Virtually every continental European nation replicates this system in one way or another. Even the United States has its National Merit Scholarships, which recognize the best students in the land. It also has a National History Day competition, privately run and financed by foundations, corporations, and trade unions, which grabs the interest of American children from elementary and high schools each year using a designated historical topic. Our failure to create such national institutions and events that reward brains is a major part of the Canadian problem.

As I have noted, there are substantial differences between provinces, each education ministry happily marching off in different directions to its own drummer. What this means in an increasingly mobile society is easy to imagine, with countless children repeating some content units and missing others as their parents move from Newfoundland to Alberta, or from Montreal to Vancouver.

When do the schools in the different provinces teach social

27

studies or Canadian history and what do they require of their students? A 1998 version of this next chart would have showed four provinces with compulsory Canadian history courses:

British Columbia

Grades 4 and 5:	Social Studies (includes Canadian "history" content, mainly Aboriginal history)
Grades 9 to 11:	Europe and North America to 1815 in grade 9; Canada from 1815 to 1914 in grade 10; and in grade 11, largely a current issues course, some historical content on the twentieth century

Alberta

Grades 1 to 9:	A new curriculum is being implemented: the grade 4 course focuses on Alberta, grade 5 on Canada; the grade 7 course has good material on pre- and post-Confederation history
Grades 10 to 12:	One course each year, depending on program stream, that covers globalization, nationalism, and practices with some Canadian content

Saskatchewan

Grades 1 to 9:   History is part of the program in grades 4, 5, 6, and 8, with much First Nations content

Grade 10:   One course required from History, Native Studies and Social Science

Grade 11 or 12:   One course required from Canadian Studies History, Canadian Studies Native Studies, and Canadian Studies Social Studies; there is some Canadian history included in the latter two areas, and a Canadian Studies course is required in grade 12

Manitoba

Grades 1 to 8:   A new curriculum is being implemented, with Canadian historical content forming a large part of the program in grades 4, 5, 6, and 7

High school: The grade 9 course Canada and the Contemporary World has small historical content, and the grade 10 course, with a global geographical focus, has very little

29

Ontario

Grades 6 to 8:   The courses in each year follow a chronological approach that covers Canadian history from the Vikings to 1914

| Grade 10: | The compulsory course focuses on Canada since 1914 |
| Grades 11 and 12: | Optional courses include Canadian History and Politics since 1945 and Canada: History, Identity and Culture |

Quebec

| Cycles 2 and 3: (Grades 3 to 6) | The courses cover white–Aboriginal contact, French and Canadian society in New France to 1745, and, in Cycle 3, Canadian society to 1820, Quebec, Prairie, and west-coast society to 1905, and Quebec, Inuit, and Mi'kmaq society to 1980 |
| Grade 11: | History of Quebec and Canada, with a provincially run examination |

Atlantic Provinces

All share a common Social Studies curriculum for kindergarten through grade 9, with historical content in grades 4, 5, 7, 8, and 9; the grade 4 course is largely geographical, grade 5 includes units on Aboriginal peoples and white settlement, grade 7 has material on Canada after 1800 and on responsible government, grade 8 looks at Atlantic Canada, and the grade 9 course on Canadian identity essentially begins with the Second World War

New Brunswick

Grades 9 to 12: There is no compulsory Canadian history course; one optional course focuses on post-Confederation Canada

Nova Scotia

Grades 9 to 12: Students must complete one Canadian history course selected from Acadian History, African Canadian Studies, Gaelic Studies, Mi'kmaq Studies, and Canadian History; the last is a survey course with substantial non-historical material

Prince Edward Island

Grades 10 to 12: One or two courses from among courses that cover pre- and post-Confederation history, PEI history, and a Canadian survey

Newfoundland and Labrador

Grade 8: In lieu of Atlantic Canadian history, Newfoundland covers Newfoundland and Labrador history in grade 8

Grades 10 to 12: One course has historical content: Canadian History, a survey from 1759 to the present, and Newfoundland and Labrador History (apparently offered in grade 8)

Yukon

Yukon uses the British Columbia program of studies, adapting it as needed to emphasize First Nations culture and history.

Northwest Territories and Nunavut

These territories use the Alberta curriculum as their basis, adapting it to suit local needs and languages.

Buried somewhere in that list is whatever Canadian children learn about their own country. In Ontario, for example, the ministry's twelve Aims of History and Contemporary Studies say little about learning and much about unabashed social engineering. The first aim is that students should "develop confidence in themselves and in their ability to deal with problems in academic and everyday life and to make sound personal, educational, and career choices." This is the first goal of the teaching of history? Never fear: the ninth aim of the twelve listed is to "acquire knowledge of historical and contemporary societies in the form of facts, concepts, and generalizations."

If I read the curricula correctly—and it is, frankly, very difficult to puzzle through the bafflegab—there are two conclusions to be drawn. The first is that more and more history is being pushed into the primary schools. This seems to be good until we realize that eight- to twelve-year-olds will not be able to grasp (or retain) some of the important concepts about Canada's past. Second, as history migrates to the younger grades, it has disappeared even further from high schools. I make out three compulsory courses—not necessarily history courses—across the country, some optional courses, and many social science/civics/learn-to-take-notes-and-write-a-paragraph courses. On balance, since 1998 and the publication of the first edition of this book, the state of Canadian history in the schools has actually deteriorated. As the Dominion Institute's Rudyard Griffiths said two years ago, "Incredible as it seems, there are [seven] provinces where you can go through high school and not be required to take a single course in Canadian history." (You can also get a BA, MA, and PhD in history at almost every university in Canada without being required to take a Canadian history course, but that is a matter for discussion in another chapter.)

What does the history curriculum truly amount to? It is frankly difficult to tell without a detailed examination of the curriculum in each province and, more important, of how individual teachers tackle the courses. What is clear is that history—a chronology-based approach to the past—scarcely exists in a systematic fashion any longer outside of the primary grades, where, truthfully, it matters least. A 2004 report prepared for Historica, summarizing two studies on teaching Canadian history, concluded, "Compared to a generation ago, students do not necessarily learn about the Canadian past in conventionally organized, chronologically based history courses." What do they learn and how? "There is a clear tendency to merge history into an interdisciplinary social studies approach in which curricula are organized around themes, topics or issues." In other words, a jumble sale with no focus.

33

Local political needs predominate—look at Nova Scotia, where the curriculum in high school history has been tailored to pander to local francophones, Gaelic-speakers, Mi'kmaqs and Afro-Canadians. Who knows, who can ever determine, what variants of Canadian history emerge from those classrooms? Who knows if the Gaelic-speakers and the Afro-Canadians share even the most basic facts with the Mi'kmaqs? What we can say is that where a history course is compulsory in Canadian schools, that course will probably, but not necessarily, be Canadian history. But even where a course purports to teach about the Canadian past, it will almost certainly be larded with current events, civics, and pop sociology. No one should be surprised that Canadian students know so little about their past, or that their parents, most of whom went to school after the 1960s' revolution in education sacrificed content for the sake of the "whole child," are so poorly informed about their country.

Worse yet, some provinces are watering down the requirements still further. In Manitoba, the Progressive Conservative government of Gary Filmon reduced the number of social studies credits required from three to two. Canadian history, which had been included in the required courses, was removed, a change that provoked a testy debate in the legislature in 1995 between the education minister, Linda McIntosh, and the New Democratic Party's critic, Jean Friesen, a professional historian. McIntosh countered that Friesen was incorrect in claiming that history was being downgraded. Yes, it was true that only language arts and mathematics were to be compulsory in grade 12, but history would "receive renewed emphasis in the first ten years of schooling." "We are moving," McIntosh continued, "to a model where content that was taught in 12 years will now be taught in 10 and that [*sic*] the increased emphasis on Canadian history and social studies will take place earlier, in more detail."

This was an important debate because it mirrored what was happening all across the nation, where historical content, as evident in the listings above, was being delivered more and more in primary school. Whether students aged seven to twelve can grasp important historical concepts or whether they simply draw voyageur canoes and forts, whether twelve years of content squashed into ten will be sufficient to instill a basic understanding of the nation's past, did not seem to trouble the Manitoba education minister, though it certainly troubled Jean Friesen— as it does me. Still, it is unfair to pick on Ms. McIntosh and her government; they are typical of all ministers and all governments in Canada, whether they be Liberal, Progressive Conservative, Parti Québécois, or NDP.

The reason is clear. It is not really the ministers who make policy but the bureaucrats. The professional educators who dominate the education ministries in the provinces remain fixated on theories of progressive education, on remedying societal ills such as sexism and racism, and on making students feel good about themselves. Whatever the criticism of those who believe otherwise, content remains second to process—a distant second. Because it is, by definition, full of content, history is no priority, especially when it is compared with trendier subjects. As an editorial in the *Ottawa Citizen* put it, "generic 'serious issues' courses permit the displacement of Vimy Ridge by Brazilian rainforest logging, Sir Wilfrid Laurier by Third World child labor."

In Quebec, the same child-centred ideology prevails, but additional ideological aims are also being pressed by governments, whether they be Liberal, Parti Québécois, or, as may be likely in the near future, ADQ. What is most striking to anyone reading Quebec curricular materials is the overt stress on Quebec. The compulsory grade 11 course on the history of Quebec and Canada (a new course is apparently to be introduced in 2008) is honest enough in its title to indicate where the emphasis is to be placed; the general objectives are clearly drafted to meet the needs of students in the present context of Quebec society and to ensure that they all understand the (inevitable?) evolution of Quebec society. To judge by the curricular materials, Canadian history is merely the alien backdrop against which events in francophone Quebec occur. Scarcely any attempt is made to compare life, issues, and events in Quebec with those elsewhere in Canada. If it happened in Quebec, in other words, it's important; if it didn't, it's not—unless *les maudits Anglais* humiliated *les pauvres Québécois* yet again.

Moreover, Canada is almost always presented as a single unit, an English-speaking entity perpetually united in word, thought, and deed. After 1939, Canada all but disappears from the course of study, which focuses on events within the province. One 1997

Dominion Institute survey found that Quebec students had the lowest score in answering questions about Canadian history, but on Quebec questions or questions of special interest to French–English relations they did relatively well. What was not broken out in the poll were results in Quebec by language. Columnist William Johnson has said that English-language students fail the Quebec grade 11 history course in larger numbers than do francophones, something he attributes to a curriculum with the "systemic view of our common history implied by so many of the questions." Originally prepared in French and translated, the questions in 1997, for example, talked of "the economic and social liberation of French Canadians" and noted that Anglo-Quebeckers were imperialist "business people or employers" who opposed any recognition of the French language. The examination also stated as fact that "the federal government patriated the Constitution without Quebec's consent"—a loose interpretation, to say the least, that neglects the solid Liberal vote in Parliament for patriation. Perhaps the reason English-speaking students fail in such large numbers has more to do with the biases of the questions and the difficulty anglophone teachers have in spouting the authorized version of the past. And if francophones do well, it might be because their teachers, whose unions are heavy separatist supporters, preach the party line that Quebec has a collective history and forms a nation. The point, as the Dominion Institute survey shows, is that Quebec's policy of stressing its own history has worked, and that Quebec City's education bureaucrats have shrewdly positioned the sole compulsory Quebec and Canada history course in grade 11, aiming it at students who are likely to be eligible voters within a year.

Quebec's recommended and approved textbooks provide the underpinnings for the compulsory history course. A paper by the Université de Montréal's Monique Nemni, presented at the 1996 Learned Societies meetings, focused on the high school history texts. To cite one example:

> I find the absence of crucial words [in a section on the October Crisis of 1970 from the most widely used text] extremely interesting. Nowhere do we read that the FLQ is a group of terrorists that used bombs that killed innocent people, that [kidnapped British trade commissioner James] Cross and [Quebec Labour minister Pierre] Laporte were hostages. Laporte is not assassinated, he is simply found dead (Did he get a heart attack?). There is no blackmail, no turmoil in Montreal. The population is not scared. Nobody is found guilty, although the members of the FLQ are imprisoned and exiled. Which members of the FLQ were imprisoned or exiled? All of them, even the ones that did not take part in the abduction and assassination?

Nemni concludes that "nationalism in Quebec is not propagated in a haphazard way by individual teachers. It starts at the Ministry level, and it permeates the textbooks." Such manipulation has been so whichever party formed the government.

On the other hand, Québécois students are every bit as present-minded as students in Toronto or Calgary. They are hardly stuffed with history, any more than are students elsewhere in the country. How much propaganda permeates a youthful mind more interested in Voivod or Les Cowboys Frignants than in Dollard des Ormeaux or the patriation of the Constitution? There is, moreover, a healthy debate in the province about the way history is taught. A working group recommended to the Ministry of Education that history be a compulsory subject in all grades; the Estates-General on Education that reported in 1996 did not go so far, but it did want more stress on history; and in June 1997 the minister of education agreed to increase the history requirement. New curricula are supposed to be put in place in the very near future. All this attention suggests that historians in Quebec feel the same despair as do their colleagues in the rest of Canada, though they have had more success than their peers elsewhere—at least there remains a compulsory history course in high school. Most of the shouting, however, is directed at the pedagogical methods employed, not at the content, although the 1996 report *Se souvenir et devenir* did call for special efforts at acculturating immigrants, both children and adults. If such efforts were put into effect, there might be something there worth emulating in the rest of Canada.

The Quebec curriculum highlights the different ways that Canadian history is taught in the various regions. In Quebec, the

39

Conquest of 1759 is featured; in the west, it is touched on only lightly. The same is true for the Quiet Revolution. Yet Québécois learn little about western developments, including settlement, the rise of protest parties, and western alienation. The teaching of Canadian history in the schools, like Canada itself, is regionalized, fragmented along geographical lines. The idea that Canada is bigger than the provinces, that national issues and national projects have mattered, is scarcely mentioned. National history, the national context, is provided only incidentally. Quebec, in other words, is little different from British Columbia or Nova Scotia, except in the political aims that inspire its teaching.

In addition to the provincial spin that is put on the study of our past, other factors affect classroom learning. In virtually every city in the country, there are large numbers of recent immigrant children who speak little or no English and whose parents are not citizens. Some come from nations with similar cultures that value education and have a heritage of democratic values; increasingly, very high percentages of Canadian immigrants do not. Some of these children, their minds and emotions back in their homelands at least for the first few years, have not the slightest interest or background in Canadian history, and teachers must scramble to find ways to make the material being taught meaningful. Not surprisingly, these teachers must devote attention to English comprehension and to reading and writing skills, as well as help students adapt to North American life with all its shocks and temptations. As one elementary school teacher told me, "The reality of the

40

classrooms and schools is that many children . . . could not handle the teaching of history, as they struggle even to master Dr. Seuss books." The difficulties that teachers in the big cities face, trying to meet the ministry's and the school boards' demands while teaching children from a hundred different nations, deserve our sympathy and support.

Of course, it's not only the recent arrivals who can neither read nor write. Given declining literacy in general, and despite the most recent United Nations data that suggest that 99 percent of Canadians are literate, functional literacy is declining dramatically. Canadian-born students are all too often non-readers whose idea of education is surfing the Internet, and who seem incapable of absorbing information that is not presented in two-minute chunks with explosive graphics and volume. The result, despite the best efforts of many dedicated teachers, is a broad-brush treatment of the past that can do nothing more than teach a few skills (note taking, writing a paragraph) and a smattering of content.

The texts used in courses today, while varying widely in quality, are in general surprisingly good. Some are pitched at English as a second language students and have a simplified language base and lighter content. Others use straightforward language and present history in some depth—the most successful being glitzed up in appearance but watered down in language and detail. No textbook writer has ever been penalized in sales for underestimating student abilities, as the most popular readers in many classrooms demonstrate. The bestsellers among such books replicate a

41

TV program in print: they present brief bursts of information in a slam-bang fashion. All that's missing is sound effects—and undoubtedly the CD-ROMs are already in production to provide the explosive bursts of noise to grab the students' attention.

The texts must also pander to provincial guidelines, and it is not only Quebec that is guilty in this respect. The role of women, for example, is a popular subject with ministries of education and school boards across the country. So too are First Nations, a subject area that is taught heavily in every part of Canada. Provincial education ministries have demonstrated that political pressure works, and the leading grievor groups in Canadian society can rest easy that the next generations of Canadians will understand their past, present, and future demands.

In the social studies classes in the lower grades of the public schools, few textbooks are used; instead, picture books (along with videos and teachers' guides) carry the load. While there are many good picture books on narrow social history topics such as regionalism, women's issues, multiculturalism, and Native history, there is very little that presents political history in its broadest sense. The few books that are available, one teacher lamented, are "usually so dated and visually boring that teachers wouldn't dare attempt to use them in the classroom." Perhaps there is scope here for a publisher to seize the opportunity.

But should we blame the textbook writers? The teachers who prepare the texts (and few university professors today write for the elementary or high school market because they get so frustrated at the political correctness with which they must deal) are trying to meet the requirements that are laid down by the provincial ministries. Only in this way can they get on the list of acceptable books that may be used for instruction. In each province, committees of bureaucrats ruthlessly vet the manuscripts of texts, demanding politically correct language, insisting on adding this and deleting that, and, overall, producing the blandest of mush. It is not the textbook writers who should be blamed for whatever flaws are found in their books but the officials in the education ministries, and the ministers and premiers who direct them. I might also add that the voters who elected the politicians who have done such damage to our schools and to a generation of students are entitled to their full measure of blame.

What can be done in the face of the provincial bureaucratic know-nothings? I believe that what is needed is a major effort to establish national standards for history in our schools. To say this is far easier than to accomplish it, given the constitutional control of education vested in the provinces. Even so, every opinion survey, every study over the past thirty years, has demonstrated that Canadians want to know more about their history and heritage and are very uneasy about the ways in which the schools are teaching these subjects. There is an opportunity here, if only Ottawa had the courage to grab it.

In the United States in the early 1990s, there was a significant attempt to establish national history standards for teaching United States and world history to meet the same appalling gaps

43

in knowledge among American students that trouble me among Canadian youth. Developed at the National Center for History in the Schools, the U.S. standards provoked a storm of controversy because, critics said, they were politically correct, replete with divisive multiculturalism, and obsessed with issues (racism, McCarthyism, the mistreatment of Aboriginal peoples) that some on the left or the right always saw as anti-American. The standards were stalled, perhaps never to come forward again. The key points, however, are that history was considered important enough to be argued about; that leading scholars, commentators, and congressional representatives joined the debate; and that the way the American past was taught was recognized as critical to national development.

How different it is in Canada! There has never been an attempt to establish national standards here and, should there be, there would probably be just as little agreement as in the United States. Even though opinion polls show great uneasiness with the situation and a desire to get history back into the schools, Canadians appear to have concluded that their history is so unimportant or so divisive that it is not something worth the fighting. Yet, Canada can never be a strong nation (or even two nations) if it does not teach its past to its people. The country needs a nationally based history curriculum with its content defined for each grade, and with publishers given specific targets for their texts to meet. To protect teachers' autonomy, the teaching strategies and methods of assessment must be left to the classroom practitioners.

How might national standards for Canadian history be developed? First, they should aim to give students two things: historical understanding (or content) that can define what students know about the history of their country and the world—understanding sufficient to provide the historical perspectives required to analyze contemporary issues—and the skills necessary to evaluate evidence, develop comparative and causal analyses, and construct historical arguments on which informed decisions about contemporary life might be based.

Second, criteria must be developed to guide the specific content standards, and should include some or all of the following:

- Standards for Canadian history should be intellectually rigorous and aim to promote questioning, not passive absorption of facts.
- Standards must be founded on chronology, the only organizing method that fosters the appreciation of pattern and causality.
- Standards must stress techniques of reading, understanding, and researching the past.
- Standards should strike a balance between broader themes and the study of specific events, ideas, movements, and people.
- Standards should reflect both the country's diversity and its commonalities.
- Standards should contribute to citizenship education through the development of understanding about our common civic

45

identity and shared values, and through the analysis of major policy issues.

- Standards must address the historical roots of our democracy, the continuing development of Canada's ideals and institutions, and the struggle to narrow the gap between ideals and practices.
- Standards must reflect the global context in which Canada developed.
- Standards must include national history, as well as regional and local history, and such areas of culture as religion, science and technology, politics and government, social history, literature, and the arts.

To suggest the detailed content of Canadian history standards would be outside the scope of this book, except to say that the focus should be on the ordinary people and the leaders, on the failures and the successes of our governments and people. Given the current focus of the research, writing, and teaching of Canadian history in the universities and schools on the flaws in Canadian society, this suggestion is more radical than is at first apparent. But the criteria above, loosely derived from the standards proposed for the United States, suggest some clear directions.

The teaching of history must be intellectually rigorous, something that it currently is not. Intellectual rigour has come to be seen as élitist in our public schools, and efforts to press children to work hard, to struggle to master complex materials, are frowned on as favouring the most intelligent and fostering unhealthy competition among students. If we fail to educate the brightest of our students well, if the rich opt out of the public school system and pay the high costs involved in sending their children to private schools with supposedly higher academic standards, then we truly will have an élitist system—and a dangerous one. To stultify learning in the public school system out of a misplaced fear of élitism is a route to national suicide, and not only in the teaching of history.

History must also teach the ways to assess evidence. Students must learn how to interpret documentation, understand narrative, evaluate conflicting perspectives, and do research. Those techniques have relevance in every other aspect of education and life. But skills, however important they be, are not and cannot be made a substitute for content. There are some who argue that it scarcely matters what history is taught, so long as the right methods are learned. David Pratt told the Canadian Historical Association in 1983 that in the elementary schools, "what is of main importance in history is the skills of handling evidence . . . The names, dates, places and events are pegs on which to hang arguments and concepts concerning human ideas and motivation, conflict and synergy, justice and freedom." If there were still five compulsory history courses in the high schools, one might reasonably make this argument, but at a time when most students are exposed to only one or even a half course in Canadian history, and increasingly only in primary school, such methodological nonsense stressing process above content is simply destructive. Teach the method,

47

by all means, but we must teach content as well. Increasingly, our public and high schools have failed to do so.

Content is not mere facts, drummed into tender little minds under the relentless pounding of rote learning. Content—even the date of the Quebec Act, Confederation, or the Battle of Vimy Ridge, or the name of the first prime minister—is cultural capital, a basic requirement of life that every Canadian needs to comprehend the daily newspaper, to watch the TV news or a documentary, or to argue about politics and cast a reasonably informed vote. In an increasingly complex and immediate world, cultural capital must also include some knowledge of Europe, Africa, and Asia, too. Without some factual basis, some understanding of why Afghanis, Iraqis, or Rwandans act as they do, Canadians will never make sense of what is happening around them. A knowledge of fact and an understanding of trends form the critical elements of our society's public discourse, and if Canadians do not have cultural capital in common, the fragmentation of our society is inevitable.

The teaching of this content must be based on chronology, the basic tool of history. By putting events in order, we can begin to comprehend why, if this event happened in 1789 or 1914, that result followed in 1793 or 1919. Too much teaching in schools today takes a module of history and puts it before students to be digested, without much awareness of how it fits within a larger context. Just like Brad, to whom I referred in the preface, students can move from an examination of gender inequity in the seventeenth century to a consideration of racism in the mid-twentieth century. Such an approach can never make clear how and why events occurred, or provide a sense of the forces that directed and affected those who lived and struggled in a past era.

Nor can Canadian students begin to understand how their country developed if its history is isolated from general world history. In Ontario, grade 9 history used to be devoted to British history, a subject put in place because of imperial and pro-British nostalgia, but also and more significantly because Canada's institutions in large part sprang from British models. Over the years, educators began to argue that in a multicultural Canada, teaching British history to all students favoured one ethnic group over the others. This was foolish reasoning that ignored the historical roots of the Canadian nation, but it prevailed, with the result that British history disappeared and students no longer understand where our parliamentary system came from and how we have adapted the Westminster model—to cite a single example.

Ideally, Canadian students would all begin historical study with the history of the ancient world and follow events chronologically through to the present. They would learn how Canada grew and changed within a global context, understanding the forces that shaped the settlement of the New World, the conquest of the Aboriginal peoples, and the subsequent creation of new societies. They would understand why Canada was involved in the European wars from the sixteenth century through to the Second World War and in the conflicts that tore apart the former Yugoslavia.

49

They would know how Canada's relations with the United States developed in a world of changing superpowers, and they might even learn why this nation for a time played such a large role in United Nations peacekeeping. Above all, they would learn history systematically, rather than in a vague, unstructured exercise. For all its undoubted flaws, the 1960 Ontario history curriculum—and those in British Columbia, Manitoba, Nova Scotia, and every other province—went much further toward achieving these goals than anything currently offered anywhere in Canada.

I recognize that such a sensible approach (even though it is followed as a matter of course in good British public schools, but not any longer in U.K. state schools) is unlikely ever to return to Canada's educational systems. The best we can hope is that Canadian history will be taught in detail, in a chronological fashion, with continuous, clear reference to the international context in which events here occurred. Ideally, it should be taught compulsorily in the higher grades and not, as is usually the case, to eleven- to fourteen-year-olds, who are too young to grasp the real issues. The young should get history as story; the older students should begin to analyze what happened and why. Without such aims, our history becomes all but meaningless.

An effort to secure national standards is worth the effort. It might not succeed but, as in the United States, the discussion, the arguments, and the contradictory interpretations of the past that would be sure to emerge will help make Canadians understand who they are and why their past matters.

History, and especially Canadian history, must be part of the core curriculum in every province. And for those who ask "What history?" "Which history?", here's an answer from Michael Bliss, the distinguished historian recently retired from the University of Toronto. In a 2001 address, Bliss said:

> If we're studying Canadian history honestly, we have not done a very good job if we don't talk about certain key historical episodes or turning points. Have we talked about Canadian history adequately, for example, if we have not talked about the first interactions of aboriginals with Europeans? Have we talked about Canadian history adequately if we haven't considered the history of New France, if we haven't considered the Conquest, if we haven't considered the effect of the American Revolution, if we haven't considered the evolution of the Canadian economy within the shifting contexts of British trade policy, if we don't talk about the rebellions of 1837, if we don't talk about the coming of responsible government, if we don't talk about Confederation, if we don't talk about Western expansion, if we don't build the CPR, if we don't talk about Canadian contributions to the two Great Wars, if we don't talk about the depression, if we don't talk about Sir John A. Macdonald, Wilfrid Laurier, Mackenzie King, and Pierre Elliott Trudeau, if we don't

51

talk about the crises caused by Quebec nationalism from the 1960s? Have we talked about Canadian history adequately if we don't talk about bilingualism, multiculturalism, constitutional reform and the coming of the Charter of Rights? Have we talked about Canadian history adequately if we haven't talked about the realignment and integration of the Canadian economy with the American economy before and after and including the decision to enter into a free trade agreement? Most sensible people would say that these are the events integral to the anatomy and physiology of Canadian history and they have to be taught if we're going to give students a proper overview of that subject.

There is, of course, much more we can and should discuss. But Bliss is absolutely correct: if Canadian history courses at whatever level in the school and university system don't discuss the issues he cites, they are not doing the job. You will be unsurprised to learn that much of the Canadian history now taught to students fails abjectly to meet Bliss's test.

CHAPTER 3

Professing Trivia:
The Academic Historians

If provincial education departments, school boards, and history teachers have let their students and their country down, so too have universities and their professors of history. Party politics and the theories of progressive educators may have determined that schools should teach children to achieve self-respect rather than to learn anything, but in university history departments the situation is just as bleak.

Universities are curious creatures. They are almost wholly funded by the provincial governments and student tuition fees, but their paymasters have little control over what they do or how they do it. The administrations preach their autonomy and independence from the paymaster, and sometimes they even exercise it. Faculty members, unionized or not, jealously protect their right to determine the courses they teach as well as the content. In the name of "academic freedom," they study whatever they choose without fear of losing their jobs.

An ideal situation for professors: they teach the subjects they like and say what they will, arguing always that this or that body of knowledge is essential for their students to master. In truth, professors are the merest of mere mortals, and their decisions on courses and course content are reached through small-group politics and individual whim, much like the other key decisions that shape our lives. History departments usually have a chair who administers and presides; in days past, the chair was the true head of the department and could direct, but this is almost always no longer the case. The assembled faculty will decide on broad areas to be covered in the curriculum, work out what is necessary for an ordinary degree and an honours BA, and lay down the standards for graduate degrees, all subject to the overriding policies of the university.

Specialization is a critical element of university education in an era that frowns on generalists. Most universities determine the number of courses or credits that a student must have for a BA in history, but few universities go further. The history department will say, for example, that undergraduate students should take—whatever their specialty—at least one course in methodology, one course in ancient or medieval history, and one course outside the history of North America. There will be four, six, or eight history courses, depending on the institution, but almost no college will mandate that a student must study Canadian history to graduate. That would be viewed by all faculty members, especially those teaching non-Canadian subjects, as interference of the most crass kind—and besides, the students had Canadian history in elementary and high school, didn't they? As we have seen, they probably did not, but compulsory courses, and especially required Canadian courses, are almost never ordained. Incredibly, students can graduate from a Canadian university with an honours degree in history, an MA, and a PhD, without ever coming into contact with the history of their own nation.

If the student decides it is important to know the history of the society in which he or she lives, there will usually be a vast array of courses and approaches from which to choose. Even the meanest institution feels obliged to cover the basic chronology of Canadian history; even the weakest offers lecture courses with tutorials and seminars for more specialized work. But who and what determine the courses that will be offered and their content?

The details of curriculum planning are determined in meetings of the specialists. The European historians, the Americanists, and the medievalists will all decide what courses will be taught, what they will contain, and who will teach them. The Canadian specialists do this, too. In most Canadian university history departments, there are more Canadian specialists than anything else, as there should be. Most departments will have pre- and post-Confederation teachers, some will have experts on Aboriginal history, and all will have professors who teach social history, a broad area that encompasses gender studies, labour history, urban history, economic history, demographics, and ethnic and immigration history, as well as local or regional history. There may also be an expert or two in political or constitutional history—although such areas are very much out of favour—and a few universities have someone who can teach military history.

Thirty or forty years ago, the Canadianists in virtually every department would have been very differently organized. Most would have been the political and constitutional specialists, and most would have focused their research and teaching on national politics. There were biographers and experts on elections or chronological periods, and specialists on Sir John A. Macdonald or the Laurier period. A few worked intensively on Canadian–American political, diplomatic, and economic relations, or on the Canadian government in the Second World War. There were almost no professors teaching women's history or Native history, few working on the regions or the provinces, and only the beginnings of specialization in other genres. Canadian history, professionally speaking, was a backwater. As more students went overseas or to the United States to do graduate work, however, they came home with new interests and new approaches. They wanted to write about ordinary people, not the leaders, the boring old white males who dominated the traditional history. "What about the workers?" they asked, and labour history sprang up, dedicated to the writing of history that did not present the story from the viewpoint of the capitalist exploiters. "What about the women?", and women's history developed. What about the Indians, cities and towns, the Maritimes and the west, the immigrants and the sojourners, the gays and the lesbians, the businesses and the fluctuations in the business cycle? Could the quantitative techniques used in

58

the "hard" social sciences also be applied to the study of the past? Under the impact of the new, the dominance of political and constitutional history shattered, never to be restored. There can be no doubt whatsoever that these developments were long overdue.

The best example of the "new" Canadian history can be found in the introduction to the first edition of *History of the Canadian Peoples*, a popular two-volume university text whose second volume was written by Margaret Conrad and Alvin Finkel, with assistance from Veronica Strong-Boag. It is self-consciously a history of the Canadian peoples—note the politically correct use of the plural— that is deliberately intended to be about the common folk, not the kings, prime ministers, and élites. As its preface proudly states, it is a history written to counter that produced in the past by "a small élite of educated white men to be read by others like themselves." It is not a history of war and political developments "in which they and their peers participated," nor is it a history written "from the point of view of the people who dominated such events." Moreover, it is not a history written from a central Canadian perspective. Instead, this is history from the points of view of women, the working class, minorities, and regions. This is history as "an arena in which classes, ethnic groups, and individual men and women struggled to control the values that shaped their collective lives." The new history uses the new methodologies imported from geography, demography, economics, political science, sociology, anthropology, archaeology, and psychology, as well as the theoretical perspectives of Marxism, feminism, and

59

postmodernism, to produce what is claimed to be a more comprehensive portrait of Canadian society.

But, like all innovations, there can be too much of a good thing. Not surprisingly, the practitioners of the new approaches, as the introduction to *History of the Canadian Peoples* suggests, quickly developed an all-too-obvious scorn for the old ways and for their middle-class practitioners, and they fought for control in their departments and their professional associations. They achieved it.

The old was swept away almost completely. The new historians effectively and efficiently took over Canadian history, setting up new journals or assuming control of the old. They ascended to the presidencies of the scholarly associations and set up specialized associations of their own, driving out all those who did not follow the mandated approach. They rewarded themselves with the prizes and fellowships that were under the control of historians—though they did less well with awards that were controlled by more broadly based organizations. They took over the hiring processes in their departments, thus guaranteeing that they could replicate themselves at will, and they trained graduate students to do the kind of work they preached and practised. They freely denounced the political historians as second-rate, teaching unimportant subjects and publishing shoddy work.

As the old white males rallied themselves and tried to fight back, the resulting war produced heavy casualties, much bloodshed, and vast expenditures of time and effort. The political historians believed that narrative was important, that chronology mattered, and that the study of the past could not neglect the personalities of the leaders and the nations they led. The social historians had no interest in the history of the "élites" and almost none in political history, except to denounce the repressiveness of the Canadian state and its agents in business. It was far more important to study how the workers resisted industrialization, the Marxist historians claimed; to investigate how birth control was practised before the Pill, feminist historians maintained; or to document gay men's experiences in Toronto's bathhouses than to study the boring lives of prime ministers, the efforts of the Canadian Corps in the Great War, or the Quiet Revolution in Quebec. Blame had to be allocated. Canada was guilty of genocide against the Indians, the bombing of Germany, the ecological rape of the landscape, and so on. Their aim was to use history, or their version of it, to cure white males of their sense of superiority. As French intellectual Alain Finkielkraut put it, "to give other people back their pride[:] Bring down the offenders, raise up the offended."*

The struggle for the past first began in Canada in labour history. The field was small and, until about 1970, it was usually studied in a narrow focus. What was the Winnipeg General Strike

---

* Increasingly, social historians have no interest in what H.V. Nelles coldly called "the nation as a unit of analysis in social history." At York University, Nelles noted correctly, "for a decade or more, graduate students have been taught 'Western Social History'" covering all of the Western world ("American Exceptionalism: A Double-Edged Sword," *American Historical Review* 102 [June 1997]: 754n). In other words, social history is social history, and Canadian variants have no special importance or claim to be taught.

about? What kinds of trade unions organized, and why did they succeed or fail? But such issues were unimportant to the new breed of labour historians who burst upon the field. They had new questions. What were the workers thinking in 1919 as they rose as one against their oppressors? What was the value of the general strike as a weapon? These differences in approach may sound trivial, but the battle between the Marxists and the non-Marxists, the new and the old labour historians, was vicious. There was only one way to study and teach the history of labour, and any form of attack against the old and traditional historians was justified. If research grant applications were sent for appraisal to the "wrong" individual, they were assessed negatively, with sweeping critiques of methodology. Book reviews turned into personal attacks, sometimes verging on the slanderous (I had to threaten a lawsuit against an especially vituperative labour historian to get an insincere apology for his lying comments), and simple survey articles on the state of the field became great battlegrounds for the destruction of the enemy. A graduate student unlucky enough to be on the "wrong" side could expect a rough ride in examinations.

Both sides fought with vigour, but no one can compete with Marxists in slander. The old-style institutional labour historians were either driven out or left the field to seek new areas to work in. The Marxists had complete control of the labour history field, including the journals and the students, and they maintain it still, notwithstanding the discrediting of communism everywhere in the world. The universities, sheltered from the real world, continue to protect their Marxists (and, let me hasten to say, so they should).

Women's historians followed suit and launched their struggle to ensure that the history of women received its proper place. And, again, so it should. For years, women were ignored not only in the writing of Canadian history but in the teaching, too. But the effort to rectify a wrong, as always, went too far. As Roger Hall put it delicately in the *Globe and Mail*, the heart of the change effected by women's history "has been to redirect the focus of the study of human experience away from political-economic roots toward social and cultural ones." Indeed, the political-economic roots scarcely matter any longer to entire schools of Canadian historians.

At the same time, women historians pored through textbooks to determine sex equity content. One early study in 1987 reported on the results: "Researchers read each of [66] books from cover to cover, noting, by page, references to women and/or girls and to 'women's issues' such as the fight for suffrage, child and infant mortality or prohibition . . . passing references . . . were also noted by page. We then calculated the extent of sex equitable content using each reference, even those of a single word." None of the surveyed books met the requirements of the sex equity policy of the Ontario Ministry of Education, and the researchers concluded that women had been marginalized by historians. Other provinces conducted similar surveys that produced equivalent results. No one seemed to care that most of Canada's history had been made by men, however unfair that might have been, and that any overt attempt to write more women into history might distort the past.

The same story with minor or major variations occurred in other fields of Canadian history, as ethnic historians, regional historians, and others counted up references and paraded their indignation. So sharp was the sense of hurt, the determination to battle against the received version of the past, that today's sensible graduate students, desperately seeking teaching posts after they get their doctorates, worry about whether to choose sides in the struggles in Canadian history or to stand aloof. Most of them appear to agree, whatever their personal decision, that fighting within and between specialties does no one any good. The all-or-nothing mindset of their compartmentalized professors horrifies and frightens them. Isn't the university a community of scholars? they ask. Shouldn't survey courses, at least, try to weave all the new perspectives, including those in political history, into a seamless web that teaches first-year students about all of Canadian history? Put in the women, the immigrants, and the workers, by all means, but why throw out the politicians, businessmen, and soldiers?

It is stunning to see the scorn in which the "old" national history is held by the practitioners of the "new." An average Canadian might think that Canada's relationship with the United States is historically important. Or Canada's foreign policy toward Britain, France, and China, to name only three nations with which we have traded in the past and with which we continue to trade. Or the development of Canada's public service, the Canadian Forces, and

64

major public policies. Or the lives and administrations of prime ministers and premiers. But such subjects are ignored by the new historians. Not only are they old hat, they pale beside the need to understand questions of labour militancy, gender, and the lives of obscure social reformers. It is somehow considered improper to study a white male prime minister, but the first Jewish dentist in Nova Scotia or an unknown female doctor in northern Alberta is worth a book. Why Canadian history should not include both the great men and the workers and women does not seem to occur to the defenders of the new history, who have revealed themselves to be far more hidebound and rigid than those they denounce. Such disputes are like theological discussions of the number of angels who can dance on the head of a pin, except that these debates are important, for they determine how Canadians understand their past. As the *Globe and Mail*'s Jeffrey Simpson said, "History departments now largely teach particularistic histories of people defined by region, locality, gender or ethnicity. Political history is considered passé in many quarters, as is history on the grand scale. Microhistory has taken over, galvanizing some, boring most." Journalist Andrew Cohen, in his book *The Unfinished Canadian*, also observed that Canada, "which has so few books on so many important topics," has somehow produced so many historians who continue to take "excursion[s] into esoterica."

How far can this particularization go? Consider the title of a paper presented at the 2006 meeting of the Canadian Historical Association, the major grouping of historians in Canada:

"Aboriginal Women as Hairdressers in Postwar Manitoba." Or this one from the same conference: "Winnipeg: One Gay City. Reconstructing a Gay and Lesbian Geography of Winnipeg." Or this: "Negotiating Sport and Gender in London, Ontario, 1920–1951." Or "The Santa Claus Parade and Urban Space in Toronto, 1920–60." What could possibly be left to examine at this level of specificity? "Jewish Electricians in North Winnipeg: A Demographic Analysis"? "Francophone Dogcatchers in Trois-Rivières, 1914"? There is nothing wrong with micro-history—unless it drives everything else out of the academy. Unfortunately, it is doing so.

The internecine debates in the historical profession inevitably have their effect on PhD students as they watch their professors wage their battles and commit their little murders. When the Canadian specialists, secure in their narrow compartments, meet in their departmental planning sessions, it is the new that dominates. One wing of the social historians fights fiercely to have more labour history than women's history taught, but only if the few surviving political historians raise their heads to plead for more do the social historians unite to swat them down.

Increasingly the old subject areas will be taught less and less, or even not at all. At virtually every university in the nation, from Memorial University in St. John's to the University of Victoria on Vancouver Island, Canadian history courses are dominated by social history, labour history, regional and Native history, and ethnic/immigration history. There will be courses in economic history, but what will be missing, or taught in one or possibly two courses, is political history. The same is true in the master's and doctoral programs all across the country—except that the specialization in courses generally tends to be even more focused than at the undergraduate level. Complicating matters—and determining the future—is that hiring has concentrated on the "hot" areas over the past twenty-five years, and there are few of the old guard remaining. Only one political historian remains in the University of Toronto's history department, for example, and he is fast approaching retirement age; when he leaves, it is highly unlikely he will be replaced.

At York University, where I taught for thirty years, there is only one active faculty member listed as a Canadian political historian—and he isn't one. There is a historian of Canadian Jewry, three who specialize in women's history, another with legal history interests, one with labour history as a specialty, another with intellectual history as a field, and two who teach fur-trade or Aboriginal history. No one does military history, foreign policy, political history, Canadian-American relations, public policy, or anything that might remotely be called national history. York University's history department was far and away the best in Canada twenty-five years ago, covering almost all the Canadian fields with superb scholars, publishers, and teachers. The present situation there is a farcical tragedy, and it is unfortunately replicated across most of the universities in eastern and central Canada.

Only in western Canada did political history courses remain in substantial numbers in university calendars. The University of Calgary's history department, the single largest and best grouping of military historians in the Western world, still offers a good range of political history courses, as does the University of Alberta.

What is clear, whatever the number of political history courses, is that national history—the history of Canada as a nation and a collectivity—is taught scarcely at all except in broad survey courses usually pitched at first- and second-year students. In the Maritimes and Quebec especially, the history of the region prevails. Even where the calendars list Post-Confederation History as a survey course, often the content will omit all but the most cursory account of national events. There are professors who brag that the names of Sir Wilfrid Laurier or Mackenzie King are never uttered in their survey courses, so fixed are they on the history of Franco-Ontarians, the history of contraceptive use and abortion, or the social history they espouse.

The result is that university graduates, like those who enter the labour force directly from high school, emerge into the marketplace culturally illiterate, ignorant of the basic details about their nation and their society that every thinking citizen requires. Yes, they may have historiographical skills that render them every bit as well trained as German, American, or French university graduates; but unlike almost all those nations' graduates, the Canadians know little about their own country's history.

Happily, there are signs that many students are not pleased with this approach. The elective social history courses are usually seminars with small numbers. Courses in political history, military history, or foreign policy, where they are still taught, are often very large and extraordinarily popular. Military history courses at the University of New Brunswick, Wilfrid Laurier University, the University of Western Ontario, and the University of Calgary continue to be pacesetters in their departments, with waiting lists for entry to some classes. The students are voting with their feet, and they seem interested in learning who John A. Macdonald was and why he drank, what Canada's involvement was in the world wars and how conscription drove French and English Canadians apart, and what role Mike Pearson played in the Suez Crisis of 1956.

Why does it matter if university students can shun their nation's history? Many of the history teachers in the primary and secondary schools and in the universities are drawn from these graduates. They teach what they know, and, in too many cases, they know nothing at all about the national history of Canada. Obviously, social history is a critical part of that history and it must be taught, but so too is national and political history. Uneducated teachers produce uneducated students.

Before this tussle between the old and the new history, historians used to be able to write for the people. Donald Creighton's biography of Macdonald is now outdated and it was written in prose that sounds florid today, but in the early 1950s his two volumes struck a chord with the literate public, who found themselves swept up in John A.'s efforts to create a nation out of fractious, far-flung colonies. Creighton's prose was stylish, if academic, but it could be read by anyone with interest in the subject—and there were tens of thousands of those.

But historians have since turned inward. Just as political scientists and economists have withdrawn from public dialogue, just as English-literature profs have deconstructed every novel and every novelist in increasingly abstruse terms, so too have most historians abandoned any idea that their task should include writing for their fellow citizens, not only for their fellow specialists. Social and economic historians discourse learnedly about their cliometric methodologies, their number-crunching techniques and regression indices, and the past and present dialectical disputes that continue to exercise them. A few of the new history practitioners have turned themselves into advocates, preaching revolution like the Marxist labour historians, or calling for the rectification of past injustices for women or Native peoples. But neither students nor general readers much care—all they know is that they can scarcely understand the graphs and equations or stilted and politically correct prose that lies on the page before them.

I have selected a few examples of this type of prose, almost randomly chosen from recent economic and social history publications by Canadian historians:

> We estimate univariate models of the price level and the exchange rate (data on Canadian interest rates are not available). We also estimate two multivariate models of the price level in which the independent

70

variables are the U.S. price level and the money stock—variables which economic theory suggests would affect the price level. In each case, the impact of the formation of the bank is tested by an analysis of the stability of the regression and by an examination of the regression residuals.

The strategies railroad families adopted for survival and well-being revealed some striking continuities. Nevertheless, there were changes as well. Married women of the first generation provided for their families' welfare through their labour in the home. A number of second-generation wives, however, also contributed as secondary wage earners. During the Great Depression, running-trades families had to abandon temporarily their emphasis on occupational inheritance as a means of providing security for the next generation.

By helping to create categories of belonging and exclusion, nationalist histories are implicated in racism. Inevitability [*sic*] they affirm the continuities between the past and present of the nation for some, and are silent on the histories of others . . . In this respect, nationalist histories contribute to the mythology that some people "naturally" belong in the country, while others are interlopers, "sojourners," or aliens. Insofar

71

as they construct their narratives from the points of view of those who are inside the nation, they also obscure the complexity of people's lives (including imagined ones) between people within and without the nation's ideological boundaries.

It was the image of Aboriginal women as immoral and corrupting influences that predominated in the non-Aboriginal society that was taking shape. Authorities used this characterization to define and treat Aboriginal women, increasingly narrowing their options and opportunities. Both informal and formal constraints served to keep Aboriginal people from the towns and settled areas of the prairies and their presence there became more and more marginal. While they may not have wished to live in the towns, their land-use patterns for a time intersected with the new order and they might have taken advantage of markets and other economic opportunities.

72

Why struggle through these thickets of unreadable prose? Why not read that novel or turn on the TV? Or why not pick up one of Pierre Berton's books of popular history and enjoy yourself for an hour or two? Berton moved into the terrain abandoned so foolishly by the academic historians, and he found broad, sweeping subjects that captured huge audiences. All were themes of national importance and national interest, and the professional historians had either abandoned them totally or written about them in such an abstruse form that only a few specialists had any interest in reading them. The field was open for Berton, Peter C. Newman, and a few dozen more journalists-turned-popular-historians. They found intrinsic interest in the stories of the Canadian past and, as they learned how to do the archival research that historians had always done, they lost none of their skill with words. Their stories leapt off the pages, captivating Canadians—and informing them. The best of the journalists became the nation's storytellers, the creators and keepers of the national mythos.

The response of professional academic historians to the intruders was predictable. The absence of footnotes was decried, the quality of the research was sneered at, and the book reviews in the academic journals were almost always devastating. I have written some reviews like this myself. Of course, academic journals almost always reviewed books a year or two after their publication, so if you were Pierre Berton and your book had already sold 100,000 copies in its first season, who cared? But on the few occasions when the journalist-historians took on the academics in debate, they usually did well, their command of the subject every bit as impressive as that of the specialists. In the *Canadian Historical Review*, Peter C. Newman, for example, absolutely savaged the historians who had attacked his treatment of Native women in his books on the Hudson's Bay Company. Newman 10, Academics 0.

I continue to believe that the nation's history is too important to be left only to journalists. The writing of first-class history about the national experience is something with which Canadian professional historians ought to be concerned. "The struggle for Canadian independence and the crises in national survival," political scientist Daniel Drache wrote, are "the great themes of Canadian history," but they do not move today's historians. Most prefer to remain alone in their specialists' cubbyholes rather than to reach out to treat subjects that tell Canadian students and citizens who they are, where they have come from, and where they are going.

In 1967 the president of the Canadian Historical Association, Richard Saunders, told his members that "a nation is a venture in history, that through an understanding of its history, it knows itself, finds confidence to be true to itself, and guidance for the future." Such words were overtly nationalist, as might have been expected in Centennial year. But such words would not often be uttered by any president thereafter; instead, it was Canadians' "limited identities," a phrase popularized in 1969 by historians Ramsay Cook (who has since largely repudiated the interpretation that became attached to his phrase) and J.M.S. Careless, that would be preached and praised. Limited identities were almost openly anti-nationalist: it was not the nation that mattered, but "smaller, differentiated provincial or regional societies"; not Canadians as a whole, but the components of the ethnic mosaic; not Canadians as a society, but Canadians in their social classes. Canadians formed a complex pluralist society but certainly not a traditional nation-state, and in that, the new Canadian historians proclaimed, lay our strength.

74

The result of this perspective, as Michael Bliss put it in 1991, was the "sundering" of Canadian history, a sundering that mirrored the fragmentation of the nation. The result we live with every day is a separatist-minded Quebec, an unhappy west, and a Charter of Rights–driven emphasis on individual or group rights. The result for Canadian history, Bliss wrote, is the apparent triumph of studies "of pork-packing, Marxist labour organizers, social control in insane asylums . . . fourth-rate nineteenth century philosophers, parish politics, and, as J.L. Granatstein recently put it, 'the history of housemaid's knee in Belleville in the 1890s.' 'Really, who cares?' he also said." I did say that, and I have been denounced for it ever since. It was an overstatement, to be sure, but it reflected my increasing uneasiness and complete frustration at the way our history is taught.

Perhaps the story is not yet terminally bleak. There are still first-rate historians who produce books of large-scale narrative, on important national themes, that achieve popular appeal. John English's biographies of Lester Pearson and Pierre Trudeau are masterful works, Michael Bliss's studies of Banting, insulin, and other aspects of medical history are superb, and other scholars such as Desmond Morton, Doug Owram, Robert Bothwell, David Bercuson, and Terry Copp have combined sound scholarship and high-quality prose to break out of the academic historians' narrow confines. They have won substantial sales and good reviews, and they study the people every bit as much as the new-style historians do, though they fit them into a broader context than the current dominant

75

cadre of social history practitioners. These scholars try to write about Canada as a nation, a people joined together by a rich history of great achievements and, yes, terrible failures. But these well-writing academics are aging, already retired or nearing their retirement to the greener pastures of being rid of their hectoring colleagues. There are, as yet, few, if any, young historians trying to join this group, perhaps because their older and younger colleagues in the university departments remain distinctly unimpressed—if it's national history, if it's readable, and if it sells, it can't be any good. As three women historians in British Columbia said, the call for the restoration of "real" history "is implicitly a call to reinstate the history of great men, male politicians, and high politics to our educational system" rather than to meet feminists' demands "for a new history which includes the experiences of women, minorities and working people." It's not, but the struggle to try to persuade these advocates of any view of the past but their own is terribly wearing.

At the root of the social historians' response is envy. The academic historians who retain an interest in national history are regularly called on as commentators on radio and television; the specialists are not, and this disparity in public attention even led a panel at a meeting of the Canadian Historical Association to bewail the unfairness of it all. Why does the CBC call the boring old white guys who work in political or military history? Why aren't the media interested in gender struggles in Montreal at the turn of the twentieth century or an obscure strike in Medicine Hat in 1918? These critics do not seem to realize that the national historians have something to say that viewers and listeners might possibly want to hear. Or simply that the researchers at the media outlets might have heard their names or have their specialties listed on their databases.

Moreover, the "academic readable" historians sell books in their thousands (the journalist popular historians sell in the tens of thousands) and might actually earn some money from their writing. The "academic unreadable" historians sell not at all and earn scarcely a penny. The standard university press run for most specialized academic history books is now about 400 to 800 copies, usually tending toward the lower end. Royalties, if they are paid at all, are in the range of 1 to 5 percent of the net price (which is list price less 40 percent), compared with the 10 to 15 percent of the list price paid by trade publishers. The price of academic books is inevitably high—usually about $80 for a hardcover history volume—and their only destination is university libraries and the author's family. Even the specialists no longer buy the books published by their peers; certainly the public does not purchase them. Naturally, the Aid to Scholarly Publications Program, which subsidizes the publication of such books with grants of $8,000 a volume, is funded by the Social Sciences and Humanities Research Council with public funds.

The vast majority of scholarly books from all the disciplines are destined to remain unread on university library shelves. How long the university presses, which also operate with the assistance of public funds, can keep on printing such dogs is unclear; if the subsidies disappear, as they eventually will, these scholarly publishers will have to adapt or die. Whether academic writers can change enough to reach readers, whether they even want to, is uncertain. There are academic historians who brag that they have no interest in writing for the public—and in whom, not surprisingly, the public has no interest at all.

The point is not that the scholarly publishing of history is unnecessary. It is vitally necessary that research into our past and present be undertaken in the universities. However, one may legitimately question the use of public funds to publish books whose only true value is to secure tenure or promotion in the universities for the authors. This unreadable sludge could be circulated to the three interested readers in *samizdat* form or made available on the Internet. To secure a subsidy, I believe a book must be able to be read and understood by those who put up the cash—you, that is, the taxpayer.

Unfortunately, the scholarly journals are, if anything, even worse than the scholarly books. Ten years ago an editorial in *Saturday Night* poked fun at the *Canadian Historical Review*, the premier journal in the field of Canadian history, and one I was the editor of in the mid-1980s: "Articles in the journal are long and turgid, as limited in scope as they are timid in judgment and questionable in relevance. The book reviews are not reviews so much as what in elementary school we called book reports—mere summaries of the contents, written without wit or reflection. Rigorous criticisms are rare, though in the current issue a scholar reviewing a text on railway regulation does puff himself up and argue definitively that 'a sentence at the bottom of page 22 should have a "not" in it.'" The editorial was right. The scholarly historians have let down the side, totally and completely, and there is no sign that the trend toward academic obfuscation will soon be reversed.

Now, it may only be a coincidence that the historical profession's turn away from national and political history took place at the same time that Canada began to fragment. Did the historians' shift to victimization and blame-seeking on the fringes, to a peoples' history, and to abstract, abstruse language lead Canada's plunge toward dissolution, or did it merely reflect what was happening in the body politic? I admit this is a chicken-and-egg question without any credible answer, but national historians of the future—if there are any and if there is still a nation—may well be fascinated by the way the trends came together. Tragically, at a time when it was critical that Canadians understand their political and constitutional history, historians wanted to talk tiny, trivial subjects of little or no general interest.

Where do we go from here? Doug Owram, one of the best of the senior generation of Canadian historians and a scholar with fine credentials in social and intellectual history, put it clearly. None of the new approaches and new theses, he wrote, have yet to achieve widespread acceptance among Canadian historians; "none can even be said to have reached the level where we can talk about a school of interpretation." Why? Perhaps it is because this nation, "so supposedly fragmented and 'limited,' has had a common historical experience of considerable duration, living under common laws, social programs, and with cultural and social ties that have national as well as local characteristics." Perhaps, Owram argued, the time has come to look at the national experience again, at "the interplay between those identities and the way in which that particular complex and dynamic interplay distinguishes this country from the rest of the world . . . The current generation of historians has shied away from any attempt at overarching interpretive frameworks. Perhaps the time has come for them to think consciously about the issue." In other words, to think of Canada as a nation, as a whole, as a society, and not simply as a collection of races, genders, regions, and classes.

The trend away from the particular in Canada has been slow to take form—far too slow. But in Britain, the United States, and Europe, national history has once again taken its proper place. Scholars and newspaper columnists, politicians and popular historians argue about the importance of the past, shout abuse at their opponents, and generally act as if the national history and the way it is written and taught matters. In the United States, there is even a category called "presidential historians," made up of good scholars who write big books on American presidents. Their subjects matter and so do the historians. The study of the great figures of the past matters—except in Canada, where the historical amnesia is all but terminal and where Canadian history as a profession is once again as backward as it was thirty-five years ago, when the labour historians started the revolution against their seniors.

"Of only one thing we may be certain," Carl Berger wrote in *The Writing of Canadian History*, "in time the new history will experience the same fate as the old history." Clio, the muse of history, he noted, "has the alarming habit of devouring those who respond to her charms." I believe that the pendulum has begun to swing—and I hope it swings to the centre, not to the other extreme, as far from the centre as is the present social history–dominated historical profession—and that new debates about our past will eventually happen in Canada, too.

CHAPTER 4

Multicultural Mania

In July 1996, the holder of the chair in Sikh Studies at the University of British Columbia gave up his position. Professor Harjot Oberoi, a Punjabi-born scholar who had held the chair since its establishment in 1987, was for all practical purposes driven from it. The reason was simple: his book on Sikh history, *The Construction of Religious Boundaries*, published by a prestigious university press, had argued that Sikhism had its roots in Hinduism and Islam. But local Sikh religious and community leaders were outraged—the Sikh faith, they believe, is both divinely inspired and completely separate from Hinduism.

A minor squabble between fundamentalists and scholars? Of course, but one with greater significance. The UBC chair in Sikh Studies was one of many chairs established at Canadian universities under the aegis of the federal government's multiculturalism program. The chair had been created with $350,000 raised from within the Sikh community and a matching grant provided by Ottawa. In other words, Canadians' tax dollars had been used to establish the post, and the outrage of a small section of the tax-paying community had been used to drive Oberoi from it. Given the violence and intimidation practised by some sections of the B.C. Sikh community—those who support an independent Sikh state in India—Oberoi's resignation probably made sense on a number of different and purely practical and personal levels.

This sad story has equivalents elsewhere. The Sikh Studies program at the University of Toronto was discontinued in the early 1990s after similar protests from fundamentalists who objected to what was being taught; the Ukrainian Studies chair at the same university, again heavily supported by federal funds, was long a focus of controversy in the 1980s; and similar tales can be told of other ethnic studies chairs in many Canadian universities. Jewish Canadians want their story told in ways that are acceptable to the community, and so do German, Chinese, Japanese, and black Canadians, among others.

So what? Every ethnic group, every religion, has an idealized version of its past. And there is nothing wrong with that. As York University political scientist Reg Whitaker put it, without the politically correct cant that dominates debate in Canada, "If religious groups want to offer money to universities for chairs in 'studies' that will prohibit genuine scholarship in favour of religious dogma, they are of course free to do so." However, any university "that wishes to retain a scholarly reputation would be advised to steer well clear of any such fool's gold." But at the University of British Columbia, Whitaker concluded, the Sikh

Studies chair was endowed by both community money and taxpayers' money. "With Dr Oberoi, we may have received value for money, but now the 'community' . . . has exercised a de facto veto placing faith ahead of scholarship . . . Multicultural mumbo jumbo aside, governments have no business throwing tax dollars into efforts by religious or cultural minorities to preen their own self-images. They can do that on their own." But Canadian governments—federal, provincial, and municipal—have been throwing money for years into multicultural education and, in the process, the history of Canada, where it is even taught, has been distorted out of all recognition. Guilt, victimhood, redress, and the avoidance of offence—those are the watchwords that rule in ethnic studies today.

It ought not to be necessary to put what follows in personal terms, but racism can be a damaging charge, and it is one that Canadians throw about very loosely these days.

I am the child of immigrants. My grandparents on my mother's side and my father escaped from a hostile, intolerant Europe and made their difficult way to Canada. Here they made new lives for themselves and their offspring, and here they slowly adapted themselves to a new culture in a new land. They suffered from racial prejudice and religious mistrust, and there was no one to tell them how the country and its government worked. Yet, they gradually (and perhaps to their surprise) found themselves becoming Canadians, attached to this best of all possible lands and part of its present and future. I was born and educated here, and I too am

87

attached to Canada, very much so. It has been, is, and will always remain God's Country to me and mine.

As the child of immigrants, I cannot in conscience be against immigration, and I am not. The glory of this nation is that its people, including even its Native people, came from somewhere else. I want this epic adventure to continue, and I believe that most Canadians, however much they fret about being overrun or worry about the numbers who flood into this country in good or hard economic times, take substantial pride in having their nation keep its doors open to the world. The race, religion, and colour bars of the past are long gone, and good riddance to them. This does not mean that Canada should exercise no controls over those who seek to come here—every country has the right and the duty to determine whom it admits—but I believe our policy toward immigrants and refugees should be as liberal as economic conditions permit. My primary concern, therefore, is not who comes to Canada, and not even how many come here.

What worries me is what happens to immigrants and refugees after they arrive on our shores. How do the Canadian people react to them? How does the state deal with them? How does it teach their children and how does it acculturate them to Canadian society? How does it prepare them to become responsible citizens with an understanding of Canada's democratic culture, secular society, laws, and government?

Does the nation tell newcomers that because they have come to a formed society they must accept its ways and adapt to its

88

norms, including academic freedom within the universities? I believe it should. Does it tell immigrants that they must leave their Old World political baggage at the water's edge? I believe it should. Does it say to newcomers that while they may keep as much of their native culture as they wish, they must pay the costs involved? I believe it should.

The aim of every Canadian and of all levels of government should be to welcome immigrants and to turn them into responsible Canadian citizens as quickly as possible by giving them the cultural knowledge they need to understand and to thrive in our society. If immigrants feel the need to associate with others like themselves and to maintain their ties to the Old Country, more power to them. But they and their communities must accept that, in Canada, political opponents and people with cultural and religious differences do not kill each other or try to censor others into silence. They must also come to understand that if they wish to honour the Old Country's ways and practices, they must do it themselves. They should pay for language and heritage instruction on their own, and not one cent of federal, provincial, or municipal government money should be devoted to fostering the retention of their cultures.

The state should spend its limited funds on helping newcomers to adapt to Canadian society by teaching them the basic knowledge, the symbols, and the ideas that literate, culturally aware Canadians understand and use to communicate with each other. To do anything else condemns immigrants to isolation, to low-paying jobs, to the expanding ghetto of the ill-paid and uneducated. Instead of practising what the Toronto Board of Education does—grafting multicultural content onto all subject areas—the schools should teach more about Canada, something that might actually be of use to the students. Teach immigrants and their children to read and speak the country's official languages; train them in the requirements of Canadian citizenship; and, where necessary, explain how a democracy functions. Increasingly, the vast majority of our immigrants comes from parts of the world where democratic government has never existed. Why should Canadians so blithely assume that our democratic values will be absorbed by osmosis and adopted at once by Pakistanis, Afghanis, Russians, Chinese, and others who grew up under autocratic, kleptocratic, or fundamentalist regimes?

At the same time as we teach democracy, we must instruct immigrants, and especially their offspring, in Canada's history and in the roots of our nationhood; give them the cultural capital that literate and aware Canadians share. Make them good Canadians, in other words. Do not turn immigrants loose to fend for themselves, to struggle alone to master the strange ways of a new and bewilderingly complex society. Do not tell them, do not even imply, that they can stay East Indian, Somali, Jamaican, German, Pakistani, Chinese, or Chilean and succeed in Canada. Their children might integrate and do well, simply because of the enormous assimilative powers of North American society, but the first generation, if they choose to remain apart, cannot.

I believe that current multiculturalism policies and use of government funds promote such separateness. This is not only a

90

shameless waste of tax dollars—one undertaken for partisan political, not national, advantage, I believe—but a terrible squander-
ing of human resources. Even worse, the policies of multiculturalism
have created the idea among immigrants (and even among native-
born citizens, especially in francophone Quebec) that Canada, and
in particular English-speaking Canada, has no culture and no
nationality of its own. If it did, they ask with some justification,
why would the government not try to show it to them? Why else
would it fund newcomers to preserve their old ways?

Canadians, of course, would have to agree on just what their
national identity is and how best to pass it on to immigrants. For
example, they have always denied that Canada is a melting pot
like the United States. Here, in the Canadian mosaic, the claim
goes, there is no imposed conformity, no national mythology, no
effort to blend all together. I think this mosaic is a myth and that
Canada is every bit as much a melting pot as the United States.
Immigrants came to the dominion in the nineteenth and twentieth centuries, learned English or French, went to school and
sang "Rule Britannia" and "The Maple Leaf Forever" until the
1950s and "O Canada" after that. They participated in school
Christmas pageants, they read from the same texts, and they
listened to the same radio programs or watched the same TV
shows. Italian, Ukrainian, Chinese, and British immigrants alike
became union members, and hockey and baseball players, and
men and women who volunteered to fight for their country in
the First and Second World Wars and in Korea. For some reason,

perhaps because we were looking for ways to differentiate ourselves from the United States, or perhaps because of our different history, Canadians pretended that there was no melting pot here. There was—though it differed in some important ways from that south of the border.

Canada certainly lacked a unifying nationalist myth that bound the country together. Though some historians argued that "Canada's nationhood was born on Vimy Ridge," they forgot that there was only a single battalion of Québécois in the Canadian Corps and that much more than half of the Canadian soldiers in that battle in 1917 had immigrated from Britain. They forgot that Lieutenant-General Sir Julian Byng, the Corps commander, was a British soldier, and so were most of his key staff officers who planned the attack on Vimy. It might have been more correct to say that English-Canadian nationalism was born on Vimy Ridge. The simple, if regrettable, truth was that French- and English-speaking Canadians had differing interpretations of the country's past, present, and future. Moreover, the colonial link to Britain meant that British monarchs and governors general, not Canadian leaders, sat at the top of the greasy pole. North American life absorbed those who came here, to be sure, but the psychic unifying force of North Americanism was substantially weaker in its Canadian variant.

There is another telling difference between the two North American societies. In the United States, major public figures have spoken out against multiculturalism and what they see as its potentially baneful effects. Arthur Schlesinger, the distinguished American historian with gilt-edged liberal Democratic credentials who died in 2007, wrote in *The Disuniting of America*:

> E pluribus unum. The United States had a brilliant solution for the inherent fragility of a multiethnic society: the creation of a brand-new national identity, carried forward by individuals who, in forsaking old loyalties and joining to make new lives, melted away ethnic differences. Those intrepid Europeans . . . wanted to forget a horrid past and to embrace a hopeful future. They expected to become Americans . . . The point of America was not to preserve old cultures, but to forge a new American culture.

Idealized view though this may have been, it was far better than what now exists. "The new ethnic gospel," Schlesinger complained,

> rejects the unifying vision of individuals from all nations melted into a new race. Its underlying philosophy is that America is not a nation of individuals at all but a nation of groups, that ethnicity is the defining experience for most Americans, that ethnic ties are permanent and indelible, and that division into ethnic communities establishes the basic structure of American society and the basic meaning of American history.

This is terribly dangerous, Schlesinger argues, because it threatens to dissolve the glue that holds the United States together. No longer is America a society of individuals making their own choices. America is becoming a society of groups fixed in their ethnic character.

Schlesinger is not alone among the intellectual heavyweights in the U.S. opposing multiculturalism. Robert Hughes, the iconoclastic Australian who has lived in the United States since 1970 and who is well known for his art criticism in *Time*, focused in his book *Culture of Complaint: The Fraying of America* on what he calls "multiculti and its discontents." He equates multiculturalism—an idea that suggests implicitly that people can live together—with the new separatism that he, like Schlesinger, sees engulfing America. He savagely belittles "Eurocentrism," the charge that higher education is dominated by the writings and ideas of dead white males. "Unhappily you do not have to listen very long . . . before sensing that, in quite a few of its proponents' minds, multiculturalism means something less than genuine curiosity about other cultural forms." To Hughes, multiculturalism means separatism, the disastrous cutting of the ties that bind America—and Western thought—together.

94

So disturbing has the rise of multicultural pressures become that Richard Rorty, a distinguished academic, felt compelled to argue in the *New York Times* in early 1994 that Americans need a national identity. Rorty denounced the proponents of multiculturalism as "unpatriotic" because they repudiated the idea of a national identity and the emotion of national pride. It is important, he argued, "to insist that a sense of shared national identity is not an evil. It is an absolutely essential component of citizenship, of any attempt to take our country and its problems seriously. There is no incompatibility between respect for cultural differences and American patriotism." Schlesinger, Hughes, and Rorty have seen the future, and they know it will not work. Europeans, suddenly aware of unassimilable and large minorities in their urban ghettos, are quickly becoming aware of this problem, too. The election of Nicolas Sarkozy as president of France in 2007 is only the first stage in what looks like it may be a very strong European backlash against immigrants and immigration.

Arthur Schlesinger looked briefly at Canada in his book on disuniting America and pronounced this country "vulnerable to schism" because Canada, unlike the United States, lacks a unique national identity. Canadians, unlike Americans, have never developed "a strong sense of what it means to be a Canadian"; instead, and wrongly, they "inclined for generous reasons to a policy of official multiculturalism."

The one certainty is that the ideal of the American melting pot as it now exists is no model for Canada. The polity in the United States seems to be in the process of breaking down. If Canadians want a melting pot, they will have to hark back to an earlier version of America. If they want to meld immigrants and ethnic groups into Canadian society, they will have to ensure that they have unifying ideas and symbols for newcomers to hold on to. In the United States of the 1900s and the 1940s, such ideas and symbols were omnipresent. In Canada, since the demise of the British connection, and especially since the advent of multiculturalism as government policy, such ideas and symbols never have been there, and we pay the price for that now.

Successive opinion polls have discovered that, while Canadians have generally warm and fuzzy feelings toward multiculturalism, they also have much dissatisfaction with the concept. A Strategic Counsel poll in August 2005 showed 69 percent wanting immigrants to integrate into Canada, and only 20 percent saying that immigrants should maintain their own identity and culture. These results were echoed by an Innovative Research Group sounding in November 2005. There is a backlash from vast numbers of conservative-minded Canadians who see multiculturalism as divisive, and who fear for social cohesion in light of the demands of ethnic and linguistic groups. The tensions are highest in urban areas where immigrants settle, but there is also fear of the future in small town and rural areas. The tiny village in Quebec that in 2006 published a list of rules for Muslim immigrants (of which it had almost none) was not alone in its concerns.

So, faced with such fears, what was the best way for Ottawa policy wonks to counter these perceptions? Not to integrate newcomers; not to teach recent arrivals in Canada about the heritage of the country to which they have come. No, the key point was that the government should promote a "new" Canadian identity based on justice, peace, and "compassionate solidarity" rather than on history and geographical considerations!

As then Liberal multiculturalism minister Hedy Fry said, multiculturalism is about "the core Canadian values of fairness and respect, compassion and equality," about building bridges between communities and individuals of all backgrounds.

In other words, more bafflegab. The federal government, the provinces, and the school boards simply fail to realize that the backlash against multiculturalism comes from the widespread realization that it will erode the history and the heritage that today's Canadians share. Canadians want justice, peace, and compassionate solidarity, to be sure, but they also instinctively believe that they have their own history and heritage. They see no reason why it should be eliminated by government fiat for a misguided policy that tries to make everyone feel good. As the teachers at one high school said, the pressure is on to teach everyone's history but our own. And so it has been for the quarter-century since the Trudeau government endorsed multiculturalism as an official policy in 1971. A decade later, the Canadian Charter of Rights and Freedoms entrenched multiculturalism in the Constitution, and, in 1987, the Canadian Multiculturalism Act expanded the concept further still. Entrenched in this way, bolstered by federal, provincial, and municipal funds, multiculturalism is an article of faith for vote-seeking politicians of all stripes and for educators. It must be defended and protected, and whatever threatens it must be rooted out—even if that threat is the teaching of Canadian history.

The only question that really matters is whether multiculturalism has been a success in nation-building—its ultimate purpose—

and, if not, can it continue? Did Canada rely too much on the huge and powerful assimilationist tendencies of North America to turn immigrants into Canadians? Has it integrated ethnic communities into the mainstream? Or, with its emphasis on the retention of cultural identities and diversity, has it allowed, perhaps even encouraged, minority identities to flourish? Has it forgotten to tell immigrants that this nation is secular, that religion and the state are separate here, and that the laws in Canada are made by Parliament, not God? Is multiculturalism a celebration of Canadianism or of nothingness? In other words, has it failed, does it fail, to create a Canadian identity and a sense of allegiance to Canada? Does multiculturalism reduce tensions in our society, or does it accentuate differences, intensify antagonisms, divide races and nationalities, and lead to ethnic communities that live separate one from the other and with no ties between them? Those are the questions we need to ask—and never do.

Consider what the Canadian left-wing social critic Naomi Klein wrote in the summer of 2005 in *The Nation*: "The brand of multiculturalism practised in Britain (and France, Germany, Canada . . .) has little to do with genuine equality. It is, instead, a Faustian bargain, struck between vote-seeking politicians and self-appointed community leaders, one that keeps ethnic minorities tucked away in state-funded peripheral ghettoes while the centres of public life remain largely unaffected by seismic shifts in the national ethnic makeup." To me, that is not an unfair description of the Canadian scene.

Canada needs and wants immigrants. But we simply must make Canadians of those who come here. Recent experience in Western Europe and elsewhere suggests that it is not enough to leave immigrants alone. We cannot let them become adapted to Canada or not as they choose, for it is all too likely that some will feel excluded from the mainstream of what they see as a decadent, immoral society and feel compelled to assert their identity—their transnational identity—as Islamists. The reality in Western Europe is that the second and third generation of Muslim citizens are more fiercely Islamist than their parents. At the same time, their sense of themselves as German or French citizens, for example, is much less strong than their identity as Muslims. The same appears to be true in Canada. As University of Toronto sociologist Jeffrey Reitz notes, "It is striking that indications of lack of integration into Canadian society are so significant for the Canadian second-born generation [of visible minorities], since it is this group which is regarded as the harbinger of the future."

So Canada has problems and, yes, racism is one of them. There is racism in Canadian society now, and there has been in the past. But Canada has never had the brutal, murderous race riots that have so disfigured American society. Our citizenship is open to everyone who lives here for three years and who qualifies, in contrast to many European nations that have a citizenship of "blood." Yet, out of a masochistic need to beat our breasts in public, Canadians try to demonstrate to themselves and the world that we are a deeply racist society. The past must be destroyed *in*

WHO KILLED CANADIAN HISTORY?

toto so that we can build anew the perfect multicultural society with the new "core Canadian values" predominant.

What do we teach children? That the Indians were the victims of white genocide and, more recently, the white appropriation of their voice. That immigrants were shamefully maltreated by Canadians and, in Quebec, that Québécois have been repeatedly humiliated by the Anglo majority that tried to assimilate them and make them fight in British wars. That blameless Ukrainian Canadians, Italian Canadians, and Japanese Canadians were interned by the federal government during the two world wars. That Canada was anti-Semitic and turned away the Jews of Europe fleeing Hitler. That blacks have been persecuted in Canada.

Much of this is true, but in history, context is all-important. Consider the internment of Ukrainians during the Great War, for example. Ukrainians in substantial numbers lived in the Old Country under the rule of the Austro-Hungarian Empire, with which the British Empire, including Canada, went to war in August 1914. The senior Ukrainian bishop in Canada at the outbreak of war urged his compatriots to be loyal to their emperor, Franz Joseph, an astonishingly ignorant and unthinking act that led to much hardship, especially for immigrants who had come to Canada for a new life in a country free of Old World hatreds. What was Ottawa to do? In a war, in a nation that was ordinarily suspicious of foreigners and especially so of "enemy aliens," fear ran rampant, and harmless Ukrainians were public scapegoats for an enemy that could not be reached. There were mistakes and stupidities aplenty in the locking up of many ordinary men in work camps, but this was not genocide. This reaction was legitimate under Canadian law and the law of war, and there is no case for financial compensation or apology. The only apology owed, in fact, was that from the bishop to his flock.

That is not how these events are presented in Canada. Ukrainian-Canadian historians and activists have campaigned skilfully for redress, for the erection of plaques to commemorate the internment of their grandfathers, and for changes in the way history is taught. To some extent, they have succeeded.

The same story can be told about Italian Canadians in the Second World War. In the 1930s, Italy's consulates in Toronto and Montreal were active hotbeds of Fascism, soliciting support and dispensing propaganda for Mussolini's regime. During the Italo-Ethiopian War, an act of naked Italian aggression against the African nation ruled by Haile Selassie that began in 1935, money was raised for the war effort, and apparently with it wedding rings donated by patriotic Italian-Canadian women. There was nothing wrong with this response—until Italy declared war against Britain and France, and hence Canada, in June 1940. Then the Fascist connections of Italian-Canadian community leaders became, not useful demonstrations of social status, but a threat to Canadian security. Many were locked up behind barbed wire at Petawawa, Ontario; and they ought to have been. They were political and financial supporters of an odious authoritarian regime with which Canada was at war, and, while they were entitled to fair treatment, they were not entitled to sympathy. Too many mistakes were made by an inefficient RCMP, and those who were wrongly sent away were owed compensation. Italian Canadians, emboldened by the success of other groups and by a sympathetic National Film Board documentary that distorted history shamefully, continue to campaign for a blanket apology and financial redress to all. They are simply not entitled to it.

Nor should Canada have recognized the huge painting on the dome of Montreal's Notre-Dame-de-la-Défense (La Difesa) church on avenue Henri-Julien as a historic site. The painting, done in the 1920s, shows Italian dictator Benito Mussolini on horseback surrounded by his admiring *capos*, all in mock-heroic poses. The painting was covered over during the Second World War, but in the new multicultural era fostered by Jean Chrétien's Liberals, it was revealed anew and declared of historic importance in 2002. Just why Italo-Canadians thought this abomination ought to have been preserved, let alone honoured, is a mystery. That more than five thousand Canadian soldiers fought and died to drive Mussolini from power and to liberate Italy didn't appear to matter when set against the burning need to recognize Italian-Canadian *amour-propre* and, more important yet, to let Liberal ministers and MPs appear to be hyper-responsive to even the most stupid of demands from their ethnic constituents. No one uttered a public word of criticism. Canada's Historic Sites and Monuments Board's members, many of them professional historians, were handed this hot potato but stoutly refused to recommend La Défense's inclusion on the list of historic sites. The politicians in the Liberal cabinet nonetheless insisted, Sheila Copps and Alfonso Gagliano leading the way. If there is a grandiose painting of Adolf Hitler in a German-language church or one of Joseph Stalin or Pol Pot or some other tinpot dictator somewhere in Canada, and if a Cabinet minister needs a few votes more, will it be next to be declared of national significance?

Then there are the Japanese Canadians, one group (like the Chinese head-tax payers two decades later) that did receive both an apology and financial compensation from Brian Mulroney's Progressive Conservative government. In the public mind today, the Japanese Canadians of 1941, all 22,000 of them, were interned after the outbreak of war in the Pacific on December 7, 1941, for no reason other than their racial origin. The Liberal government of Mackenzie King acted out of racist motives, nothing more.

This received version is both right and wrong. There is no doubt that the vast majority of Japanese Canadians posed no threat to anyone. But the Japanese consul-general in Vancouver was actively propagandizing and proselytizing among his fellow and former countrymen (all of whom were citizens under Japanese law and in Tokyo's eyes), and he was under orders to recruit spies to secure answers to a long list of questions of military significance sent from Tokyo. Incriminating telegrams directing such activities were decoded by Washington and were made known to Ottawa by British intelligence sources. There was also near-panic in British Columbia as the Japanese armies swept across the Pacific, and both the provincial government, local military commanders, and "vigilante" groups were demanding action. In February 1942 Ottawa gave in to the pressures and ordered the evacuation—not internment—of Japanese Canadians from the coast to the B.C. interior. Some seven hundred Japanese Canadians *were* interned at Angler in northern Ontario, but these men were deemed threats to Canadian security or were self-declared supporters of the Japanese Empire.

This rough justice ruined lives and destroyed many Japanese Canadians financially. But there was a war on, there was a real fear of attack and even invasion, and Japanese fifth-columnists had already demonstrated how devastatingly effective they could be throughout Asia, including at Hong Kong, where an understrength brigade of Canadians was killed or captured. At the least, Ottawa's actions can be defended as driven by militarily necessary. What cannot be justified was the judicial theft of Japanese-Canadian property, a shameful event in Canadian history; thousands scrambled to pick up the property and belongings of the evacuees for a song. For this loss, Japanese Canadians were justly entitled to compensation, and a postwar royal commission (inadequately) gave it to them. For the evacuation, no apology was needed. Even democracies have the right to defend themselves. In early 1942, with the war going very badly, Ottawa, its military commanders in the Pacific, the government in Victoria, and the overwhelming majority of the British Columbia population believed Canada had to act. As it turned out, there was no attack on the west coast, aside from a single submarine shelling the Estevan Point lighthouse—but no one knew this in February 1942.

The postwar Japanese-Canadian community lobbied long and hard for redress and finally won it. I believe the Mulroney government's action was half right, but governments should not try to alter history's decisions. If they do, they owe the past the courtesy of explaining why decisions were made. In the climate of the 1980s, in the atmosphere of multiculturalism, victimhood, and guilt, no such explanations were offered. Canadians were told only that their forebears had acted brutally in a racialist way, that there was no military threat and no danger of espionage, and that internment (*sic*, for "evacuation") was completely unjustified. Well, yes and no.

So strong was the desire among good liberal-minded Canadians to embrace guilt that anyone who questioned the apology and redress to Japanese Canadians was de facto a bigot. When I wrote a *Saturday Night* article on the history behind the issue and published a subsequent book (with Masako Iino and Hiroko Takamura, two Japanese historians, and Patricia Roy, a British Columbia historian), I was subjected to the worst barracking I have ever received. I was as racist as was the government in 1942 (I wasn't), my facts were incorrect (they weren't), and surely I could see that the government's interning (*sic*) of Japanese Canadians on purely racial grounds was the moral equivalent of the Holocaust. No, it wasn't—not even close. In the context of 1942, there was reason to fear the loyalty of British Columbia Japanese, there was reason to believe that Japan had agents at work, and there was reason to believe that the very weak units of the Canadian army in B.C. might have difficulty

105

protecting Japanese Canadians against the possible attacks of other Canadians. All these statements are defensible, soundly based on evidence, and all but irrefutable. But they clashed with the culture of victimization and the desire of many Canadians to believe that they were just as guilty of racial sins as was any Nazi.

The Mulroney redress precedent, of course, emboldened every other ethnic group. As Columbia University historian Alan Brinkley said of the United States, where the mania for apologies is as widespread as in Canada,

> There are occasions when a government has been complicit in the commission of some grand wrong, the obscuring of it or both. And in those cases, an apology might be appropriate. It would, for instance, be a great thing for the Turkish government to apologize for the massacre of the Armenians—even though they were not the government in power then—because it continues to be officially denied. But, as a rule, if government is going to apologize, it should be for something it did rather than something that happened 100 years ago. And even then the consequences may well be perverse, opening the door to all kinds of frivolous demands and unresolvable controversies.

Brinkley was right. After the Japanese Canadians secured their redress, diverse other groups pressed their cases for apologies for the sins of past policy from which they had suffered. Undoubtedly, thousands were treated shamefully throughout history, from the deportation of the Acadians, to the head tax on the Chinese, to the abuse of Indian children in residential schools, to the immigration department's turning away of Jewish refugees, and to discrimination against present-day Somalis in Toronto. But apologies and victimhood do not make for either good current policy or a proper collective understanding of history. Instead, they create cynicism in the silent majority of Canadians who are convinced that certain groups are trying to rip off public funds.

We all are aware that Canadians have sometimes acted shamefully. But Canadians in their five hundred years in this most favoured of lands have committed relatively few atrocities when compared with virtually any other society. There are no Bosnian, Serbian, or Croatian massacres in our past, no Armenian genocides, no Christian crusades or Muslim jihads. Canadians have fought and argued, cheated and stolen land, hated and feared, but ordinarily they have done so in relatively contained and constrained ways. We should know about the appalling episodes in our past, and we must try to learn from them. But to pretend that Canada has been and remains a monstrous regime with blood-stained hands, to suggest that Canadian history is one of brutal expropriation, genocidal behaviour, and rampant racism, simply will not wash.

Tell that to the elementary and high schools. Ontario's appalling 1993 Guidelines for Ethnocultural Equity in School Boards, put in place by Premier Bob Rae's NDP government, complained that

107

"Ontario's school system has been and continues to be mainly European in perspective. The prevalence of one cultural tradition limits students' opportunities to benefit from the contributions of people from a variety of backgrounds." The guidelines went on to say that "exclusion of the experiences, values, and viewpoints of Aboriginal and racial and ethnocultural minority groups constitutes a systemic barrier to success for students from those groups and often produces inequitable outcomes for them." The government's Resource Guide for Antiracist and Ethnocultural Equity Education (1992) made the point that the province's schools, because they have been Western European in content and perspective, have left students of other backgrounds believing that they have not been "represented in Canadian history" or not "represented positively. This failure of the system to give equal attention and respect to all groups has contributed to stereotyping." In other words, sugar-coat everything that is not positive for every non-white group and for immigrants other than those from northern Europe. The Rae guidelines were drastically watered down by the Harris Progressive Conservative government, but their spirit survived.

108

On one level, the impact of such policy was that schools no longer felt able to celebrate a holiday such as Christmas unless they did the same for Muslim, Jewish, and Buddhist festivals and the recently invented (1966) black holiday of Kwanzaa. This reaction, silly though it be, drastically shortchanges all Canadians. Our civilization and culture is Western and Christian, and there is no reason we should be ashamed of it or not wish to teach our students about it. Canadians are the inheritors of Greek and Roman traditions and the British and French experience, and the West is the dominant civilization in the world today in part because its values have been tested and found true. To pretend that a simple relativism should apply in the schools and that immigrants, who have come here because they want to buy into our civilization and value system, should be told to retain their own culture is wrong-headed in the extreme. It also discriminates against newcomers by systemically patronizing and marginalizing them.

If only the rest of our history were taught and the racist interludes were presented in context, one might barely tolerate this perversion of fact. But it is not. To present university students with an article on the Japanese Canadians and to pretend that this one slice covers the national experience of the Second World War is a grotesque distortion, a complete absence of context. To use this same example in a primary or high school history class with students who know nothing about the war, including which side Canada was on, is even worse. Yet, if presented with it in context, students in high school and in university could benefit from this lesson: how a war fought against Nazi racialist beliefs was marred by Canadian racism.

What this multicultural and antiracism emphasis on grievances has done is to reduce history to "a treasure-trove of incidents and examples which were used only to illuminate some present concern." Often, wrote Ken Osborne, a student of the Canadian schools' history curricula, "history disappeared as a course, to be replaced by a kind of mini-anthropology of Canada's constituent cultures. Multiculturalism painted Canada as a community of communities, but its emphasis was on the plural rather than the singular . . . the final result was usually a series of discrete but mutually isolated heritages, united only by being located in the same political unit."

Let me try to be as clear as I can be: I do not want children to be taught an airbrushed history of Canada with all the warts removed. I do not want the experiences and contributions of non-Western cultures to be banned from the schools. Nor do I want a curriculum that is relentlessly political history, one that focuses on the "great men." What I want is what the schools and the nation need: a history that puts Canada up front, that points to the successes and failures of our past policies, and that gives due weight to the contributions made by non-charter-group Canadians. I want a history that puts Canada firmly in the context of Western civilization, but gives full weight to the non-Western world. I want a history that recognizes what men and women, great and ordinary, did to build a successful nation. I want frankly what every sensible Canadian, native-born or immigrant, should want: that the truth about the Canadian past be presented to our young people.

Sometimes the pursuit of political correctness becomes ridiculous. The statue of Samuel de Champlain on Nepean Point overlooking the Ottawa River in the nation's capital, for example, was denounced for its presentation of Native Canadians. Champlain stood proudly atop the plinth, while below him knelt a Native. It mattered not at all that the statue was a hundred years old. In the eyes of organized Native groups, it was demeaning, and there was strong pressure—ultimately not successful—to remove the figure of the Indian. There was no unanimity among Native leaders, however. One from the Rama First Nation band said, "What we would like to do is use the statue and learn from it . . . Removing the figures and storing them in a warehouse . . . doesn't make sense. Isn't that what they did to Indians in the first place?"

Or consider the brief rediscovery of Clara Brett Martin. The first female lawyer in Canada and Ontario, she persevered against gender discrimination and was called to the bar in 1897. Feminist legal historian Constance Backhouse, a writer who made no effort to hide the fact that she had consciously set out to create feminist heroines, declared her an archetype, and soon universities named lecture series and research centres after her, and the Ontario government dubbed its attorney-general's main office building in her honour. All well and good, except that a diligent legal researcher discovered that Brett Martin was anti-Semitic in her attitudes and actions as a Toronto property owner, and Robert Martin, a legal columnist and law professor emeritus at the University of Western Ontario, publicized the story. Poor Clara, so recently rediscovered, was interred again in ignominy. Again, historical context was totally absent. In the early twentieth century, anti-Semitism was common, indeed accepted, in Canada, the United States, Britain, and Western Europe. It was not right, but it was present,

111

and Brett Martin was simply a woman of her era, though one more courageous and determined than most of her peers. Political correctness had motivated her sanctification, and political correctness led to her subsequent demonization. Those who are brought to life again only because of the abuse and misreading of history apparently are doomed once more to perish by it.

My point is, or should be, simple: history happened. The object is not to undo it, distort it, or to make it fit our present political attitudes. The object of history, which each generation properly interprets anew, is to understand what happened and why. A multicultural Canada can and should look at its past with fresh eyes. It should, for example, study how the Ukrainians came to Canada, how they were treated, how they lived, sometimes suffered, ultimately prospered, and became Canadians. What historians should not do is to recreate history to make it serve present purposes. They should not obscure or reshape events to make them fit political agendas. They should not declare whole areas of the past off-limits because they can only be presented in politically unfashionable terms any more than they should fail to draw object lessons from a past that was frequently less than pleasant and less than honourable.

112

Because the past was not perfect, it must not be made perfect today. Yes, students should not be exposed to prejudicial references in their texts. It does no one any good to refer to Indians as savages (though that was how their white contemporaries described them from the sixteenth century on) or to teach gender inequality and racial superiority. But our past is littered with these usages, and the danger exists—and, as we have seen, it is very real—that a worthy present requirement can quickly begin to distort what happened in the past. And so it has. "We can become so afraid of offending anyone," said retired McMaster University historian John Trueman, "that we end up satisfying no one." The result is that "history as we have known it and taught it will simply cease to exist in the schools."

Not only were school curricula to be swept clean of any "offensive" materials, but the actual learning environment was to be monitored. In Ontario, for example, Bob Rae's NDP government, the most perfectly Politically Correct government in Canadian history, adopted a policy of "zero tolerance" of discrimination and harassment in the universities. Successor governments turned the policy into one that aimed to end violence in the schools, a measure that was instantly assailed as anti-black. In 2007, the Ontario Liberal government watered the measure down. The original Rae policy aimed to protect students against discrimination because of race, creed, sex, sexual orientation, disability, age, dialect, and accent. Harassment, however, was defined as "something that is known or might reasonably be known to be offensive, hostile, and inappropriate." Another offence was the creation of a "negative environment," and "a complainant does not have to be a direct target to be adversely affected by a negative environment."

The impact of such a policy on a university classroom should be obvious. If I were a student of German origin in a course studying the Holocaust, could I not reasonably feel the victim of a negative

113

environment? An Iraqi-born student in a class on the present Middle East? A Chinese immigrant in a class on the Korean War? Or a Québécois in a class studying federalism? How easy it could be to make a student feel marginalized, excluded, harassed, the victim of a negative environment. That students might learn from having inherent prejudices challenged did not occur to the Rae government.

If this hostile approach to untrammelled learning existed—it still exists in the universities—how much stronger was it in the elementary and high schools of Ontario? The Toronto Board of Education in 1994 produced a policy statement on "racial and ethnocultural mistreatment" that defined a negative environment as the product of "acts or omissions that maintain offensive, hostile or intimidating climates for study or work for individuals or groups." Such an environment was "characterized by inappropriate choices in, or lack of attention to, a racially and culturally inclusive and equitable curriculum and pedagogy." In other words, every teacher was on notice to be very careful that course content did not upset students and their parents. There would be no "stereotyping and bias in curriculum and pedagogy," no "historical and factual misrepresentations." If only one ethnic group's facts were the same as another's. Of course, they are not. If you doubt that this is so, talk to Canadian Croats or Canadian Serbs about recent Yugoslav history or about events five hundred to a thousand years ago. The singularity of ethnic interpretation of the recent or distant past is all too clear.

Ontario was the clearest example of this trend in Canada, but the other provinces in their own disparate ways were moving in the same direction. All attempted to remove anything "offensive," for whatever reason, from school curricula and learning materials, and all committed themselves to introduce positive materials about minorities, their cultures, and their past, present, and future contributions to the nation. All worked to train teachers and principals, and, as one federally financed course offered in Toronto put it, "to reduce principal and teacher resistance to multicultural and anti-racist education."

Because our own history has been so neglected, inevitably American culture, carried by TV, movies, magazines, and clothes, sweeps all before it. Walt Disney is the cultural norm for students, the master of past and present, and Bart Simpson the exemplar. Canadian students probably know more American history than Canadian. As political scientist Gad Horowitz lamented the passing of Canada, "Multiculturalism is the masochistic celebration of Canadian nothingness."

CHAPTER 5

No Flanders Fields?
Canadians, War, and
Remembrance

I had the opportunity of attending the fiftieth anniversary celebrations of D-Day in Normandy and London in June 1994, and the fiftieth-anniversary commemoration of V-E Day in Apeldoorn in the Netherlands and in London in May 1995 with the Canadian Broadcasting Corporation. These were astonishing, wrenchingly emotional events that left me and many of those who participated in them in tears much of the time. To watch the old men, once young, march through the streets of Courseulles, St. Aubin, and Apeldoorn, Amsterdam, Groningen, and fifty small Dutch towns was to realize how quickly time passes, how soon we are old. The two commemorative events also made many Canadians aware again how little, in contrast to Western Europeans, Canadians know of what their soldiers did in the Second World War.

The Dutch certainly know of the First Canadian Army. In May 1995 in the Netherlands, the one country in the world where Canadians are universally hailed as liberators, every house was decorated in the colours of the House of Orange and with Canadian flags. Homemade banners, obviously erected by ordinary citizens or neighbourhood associations and not by the state or munici- palities, seemed to stretch across every street. I especially remem- ber the theme of gratitude, written in English on one banner in Apeldoorn, that was clear to all: "Bless You, Boys."

The Dutch remember the war. They remember the brutality of the Nazi occupation, the starvation winter of 1944–45, the executions of resistance fighters that went on into May 1945, and the collaboration of many of their men and women with the oppressors. They remember, but they no longer hate the Germans, with whom they willingly cooperate in a combined German– Dutch corps in NATO. They remember, above all, those who fought and died to liberate them, those men of the First Cana- dian Army who came from afar to drive the Germans out of Holland, those RCAF pilots who supported the armies and dropped food to them in the hungry days just before liberation, and the RCN sailors who cleared mines and ferried supplies.

Their acts of remembrance were visible in the Canadian war cemeteries at Groesbeek and Holten, both of which are supremely beautiful places, if one can say such a thing of graveyards where thousands of our countrymen are buried so far from home. At Holten, several days before V-E Day, there were perhaps a hundred ordinary Dutch families wandering among the endless rows of head- stones that—beneath a carved maple leaf—list the rank, name, dates of birth and death, regiment or corps, and sometimes a message from parents, wives, or children. I didn't understand the words that

120

the children were hearing, but I was sure that I could catch the message: these men, these boys—and so many of them were boys who had the demographic bad luck to be born in the 1920s and to grow up knowing little else but the Depression and war—had died to free your nation from oppression. Do not forget what they did for your country. Remember that you are free because of them.

Those Canadians who assume that the liberation of Holland was a cakewalk against a beaten Wehrmacht would be disabused of that notion by the five thousand soldiers, many of them killed in fighting in Germany, to be sure, who are buried in these war cemeteries. At Holten, for example, there are twenty men of the Cape Breton Highlanders whose headstones reveal they were killed in action on May 1, 1945, in liberating the little port of Delfzijl, a battle that their regimental history calls its hardest fight of the war. On May 1—with Hitler already a suicide and the war inexorably drawing to its close! The Dutch families at Holten that day understood what their liberation had cost.

The same public display of memory was evident for all to see—including a huge CBC television audience—in the amazing victory parade of Canadians through Apeldoorn, a few days before the V-E Day anniversary. Apeldoorn is a pleasant town of about 100,000 people in central Holland, quiet, staid in the reserved Dutch way. But that day, just as fifty years before when the Canadian Shermans rolled into their towns, the Dutch were far from staid. In May 1995 Apeldoorn's streets were lined by at least a half-million men and women, children, and babes in arms. The 15,000

121

or so Canadian vets who marched through the streets were mobbed, showered with kisses, handed drinks, smokes, and flags in a sincere outpouring of love, affection, and gratitude. The parade, scheduled to run for about two hours, lasted for eight, so slow was the triumphal progress through the happy crowds. That the vets lasted so long was a tribute to the power of exhilaration to overcome the aches and pains inherent in seventy-five-year-old bodies.

I will never forget the sight of young mothers in their twenties, weeping and cheering simultaneously while holding their babies up to get a sobbing veteran's kiss. The Dutch mothers told the cynical and astonished Canadian reporters they were doing this so their children could say they had been touched by one of the men who liberated the Netherlands a half-century before.

The Dutch remember. They teach their children about the war in their schools; they teach that freedom is everything and that, if not defended, it can be lost. They take whole schools to the Canadian cemeteries each year to light candles and to lay flowers on the graves and to make the point that the preservation of freedom has a price.

How different it has been in Canada. The Second World War was a time of supreme national effort for Canadians, who produced a military, industrial, and agricultural contribution to victory that was frankly astonishing. Ten percent of the population was in uniform; Canadian war production, starting from effectively nothing, became large enough for us to give to our allies billions of dollars worth of weapons and foodstuffs—on a proportionate scale a greater amount than that of the United States. There was scarcely a family in the land that did not have someone in the service, either as a volunteer, as were the vast majority, or as a conscript. There is no doubt, however, that the war was fought in large measure by Canadians of British origin.

This fact may partly explain the curious way we study—or do not study—the war in our schools. In this new multicultural Canada, the history of the world wars is seen as a divisive force, something that is almost too dangerous to teach in primary and secondary schools. What might a child of German or Slovakian or Croatian origin think, how might the youngster feel, if the Second World War was discussed in any detail? Better to say nothing, or look at the war only in terms of its impact on female workers in munitions plants, or stress the unjust way Canada treated Japanese Canadians or barred Jewish refugees fleeing from Hitler. The pride that Canadians should feel in their substantial role in the war, the lessons its events should hold for us, are brushed aside by the efforts to create a history that suits the misguided ideas of contemporary Canada held by successive federal and provincial governments and by far too many academics.

"Freedom's just another word for nothing left to lose," a once-popular song put it, and certainly that is how Canadian schools and universities treat it in their avoidance of our war history. But the song is dead wrong: freedom is the word for what is most precious, for what cannot be lost, a word and a concept for which so many Canadians fought and too many died. The children and

123

grandchildren of the Dutch who lived through the war and brutal occupation understand this and remember what can happen if freedom is lost; pathetically, terribly, the children and grand-children of those who liberated them do not.

The veterans still remember. They had become inured to public indifference, to sincere, well-meaning, but largely unattended ceremonies on Remembrance Day, and to the small crowds that celebrated the events of 1939 to 1945. Still, the celebrations of the milestones of the war—the fiftieth-anniversary commemorations of the Battle of Britain, the Battle of the Atlantic, the D-Day inva-sion, and V-E Day (the Italian campaign was largely neglected, just as it was during the war!)—were critically important to the vets. How fortunate that the Dutch knew how to sing their praises, even if most Canadians did not.

Perhaps that stirred some guilty feelings in Canadians. After the D-Day and V-E Day commemorations abroad, attendance at Remembrance Day ceremonies began to increase. The crowds at the National War Memorial each November 11 grew larger, the television audiences bigger. The Royal Canadian Legion began to press for Remembrance *Week*, the newspapers and electronic media to give much more coverage to stories of and by those who had served. The arrival of History Television on Canadian cable TV added to the mix, with an endless stream of documentaries, some good, some not, that led some to call the channel the "World War II network." The advent of the World Wide Web added to the

124

mix with information on individuals, units, battles, and militaria readily becoming accessible to all.

Then the Canadian War Museum's troubles entered into the mix. The idea of adding a Holocaust gallery to the museum's old building on Sussex Drive in Ottawa stirred up a furor in the mid-1990s. It was not that the Holocaust ought not to be presented, angry veterans said, but that the Canadian role in the world wars and post-1945 conflicts had to be adequately presented first. A parliamentary inquiry put paid to the idea of a Holocaust gallery, there were resignations among museum officials, and the idea of a new War Museum began to percolate. Then the Legion's long campaign to repatriate a Canadian unknown soldier and to inter the remains at the National War Memorial gathered force. In 2000, finally, it was done in a moving ceremony attended by thousands and watched by millions.

Sparked by this new interest in their youthful battles, vets, it seemed, began to talk to their children and grandchildren about their war experiences. This cannot be documented, of course, but there are enough accounts of this occurring to suggest it must be so. Old men were telling their stories, speaking about old wounds to the body and the psyche and remembering the good and bad times of the war. The fog of war had begun to lift and the public memory to be stirred.

Why were we so ignorant? The lamentable failure of our schools in treating the wars—and all of Canadian history—was a large part of it. This neglect began in the universities, for it is the university history departments that train most of the history teachers for primary and secondary classrooms. First, it is important to understand that military history is not taught in most Canadian universities, the University of Calgary being the one major exception. Canada is not alone in this—Harvard University has no specialist in military history among its fifty-eight historians—but it may be that the situation is worse in Canada. This absence of Canadian expertise can lead to some extraordinary howlers in the work produced by non-experts and those who think that fact-checking is unnecessary.

Let me begin by considering the account of the two world wars in the first edition of *History of the Canadian Peoples*, the best-selling university text already referred to in Chapter 3. The account of the Great War focuses on the conscription election of 1917; the actual fighting receives only six short paragraphs and a half-page sidebar. The account of trench warfare is essentially correct, though the number of casualties, and especially those wounded in action, is misstated. The most extraordinary aspect of the few words on the war is in the sidebar "'Manpower' and the War." The military's "exclusionary" policies are denounced for increasing the shortage of soldiers for the front: "Despite the eagerness of some women to serve overseas," we are told, "they were unwelcome on the front lines." Women were permitted to serve only as nurses, and forty-seven died, "victims of enemy attack and disease contracted from patients." When non-white males volunteered, "they, too, were often turned away" because they might "offend the racist sensibilities of the men at the front." Some of this is correct, but to suggest that Canada could have welcomed female soldiers for front-line service is simply bizarre. The attitudes and culture of 1917 Canada simply would not have permitted it; no government on either side of the war allowed women to fight as combatants. How the textbook's authors could not know this, how they could write as they did, is unclear—unless they were determined to flaunt their present-day feminist credentials and to emphasize the anti-female attitudes of a male, white government even to the point of grossly misrepresenting history.

When the *History of the Canadian Peoples* turns to the Second World War, we begin with a capsule treatment of the conscription issue that is unexceptional. Then we are told that while Prime Minister Mackenzie King resisted pressures in favour of conscription, "he was unwilling to reduce Canada's commitment to the Allied war effort," a phrasing that must be intended to suggest he should have done so. This "failure" appears to be responsible for the decision in November 1944 to send home-defence conscripts overseas, a decision that provoked mutinies in camps in British Columbia. Nothing is said to suggest that the lack of infantry reinforcements was leading to higher casualties among units fighting in Italy and north-west Europe. The implication is that a capricious government, neglecting the impressive French-Canadian contribution to the war, acted unthinkingly and, as a result, "strengthened the credibility of

127

WHO KILLED CANADIAN HISTORY?

Quebec nationalists and added to feelings of betrayal among French Canadians." Clearly, that the soldiers overseas might have felt betrayed if they were not reinforced never enters the authors' minds.

The text then gives incorrect numbers on enlistment in the three services, and in one brief paragraph treats the war fronts on which Canadians served: "In December 1941, Canadian forces were involved in a futile attempt to dislodge the Japanese from the British colony of Hong Kong," a wording that implies that the Canadians were invading rather than defending the island— as they were. The Dieppe debacle is mentioned, with casualty figures, closing with a bald statement that ends the paragraph: "Canadians also participated in the liberation of Europe, including the invasions of Sicily in 1943 and Normandy in 1944." So much for the efforts of the First Canadian Army, the RCAF, and the Royal Canadian Navy in liberating Europe.

We then get a longer paragraph than the preceding one on women's role in the armed forces ("Although only men participated in combat, 43,000 [the correct number is more than 50,000] women in uniform worked behind the lines"), and a longer one still on wartime civil rights abuses in Canada. German and Italian Canadians were "imprisoned without trial . . . on the basis of flimsy evidence connecting them to the Nazis or fascists," we are told. That there were active Nazi and Italian Fascist groups in Canada and that they had been spreading propaganda and raising money for their masters in Berlin and Rome does not make it into the story; rather, the impression is deliberately established that the government was again acting capriciously and brutally. The Japanese-Canadian story is told somewhat more fairly: the authors at least recognize, as some other texts do not, that the Japanese Canadians were evacuated from the west coast, not interned, and that some Japanese Canadians might have been disloyal.

What impression might a university student take away from these accounts of the world wars? Canada's governments were over-committed to the fighting; they acted brutally toward and discriminated against women, ethnic Canadians, and racial minorities, and trampled underfoot the rights of French Canadians; and the contribution to the fighting by Canadians in the Second World War was insignificant except for the Hong Kong and Dieppe defeats. To say that such accounts view the war through a distorted lens is surely an understatement. What makes this distortion all the more extraordinary is that the two world wars were genuine "people's" wars for Canadians, calling forth extraordinary efforts from men and women both overseas and at home. No other events of the twentieth century had a greater impact on Canada, but the authors of the *History of the Canadian Peoples* are so intent on painting a tale of prejudice, bias, maltreatment, and discrimination that they almost completely omit the people they claim to be chronicling. To be fair to the authors, some of their errors have been rectified in later editions. What is significant, however, are the attitudes expressed and the blinkers revealed in the first edition. The text there says what the authors think; their corrections and additions merely demonstrate what they were willing to do to hold their market share.

129

Other university texts are surprisingly similar in approach. They will have a page or sometimes only a paragraph on the fighting at the front in each war, but invariably the emphasis is on the troubles of the home front. University history "readers" that collect articles for classroom discussion and are designed to accompany textbooks almost never have any coverage of fighting overseas, most of the space being devoted to the mistreatment of minorities or women's role in factories. It is, as more than one writer has noted, part of a concerted effort to create a Canada out of ideological fantasy—a Canada dedicated to caring, neutrality, and peacekeeping.

The attitude that underlies the mistreatment of the history of the wars derived from a reaction against "certain assumptions about human nature which excuse or justify competition and aggression." Queen's University's Katherine McKenna wrote in 1989 of being baffled "by the almost universal viewpoint my students have expressed about the naturalness of conflict between people. War, they have told me, is inevitable. Peace is idealistic, utopian and unnatural." Why should students feel this way? Because, she continues, in most school courses "the traditional emphasis on wars and political conflict as the driving forces of history remains intact"—something I might suggest is no longer even remotely true. If only women had shaped history—"their activities," McKenna said, "for the most part have historically been more nurturant and co-operative." Cooperation and peace should be taught, McKenna went on, although these are the attitudes students see as weak and unrealistic because they have been "taught a biased view of history and human nature." This condemnatory approach to the way history has been written (and the way history has been made!) has certainly captured most present-day textbook writers, male and female, and it probably explains why the fighting has been all but eliminated from the Canadian history of the world wars.

It also explains why peacekeeping, a useful modern specialty of Canada's armed forces, has been elevated into an almost sanctified principle of Canadian nationhood. Peacekeeping is the traditional Canadian military activity, we are told on television, in the press, before parliamentary committees, and increasingly in the textbooks used in schools. The sole national military monument erected since the Second World War commemorates the efforts and sacrifices of Canadian peacekeepers—and so it should. But peacekeeping, however helpful it may be (and there is substantial doubt about its effectiveness in Cyprus, the Middle East, Somalia, the former Yugoslavia, Rwanda, the Congo, and elsewhere), can be only one small part of this country's military role. Professor McKenna undoubtedly admires peacekeeping because it counters the ideas of male aggressiveness she rightly abhors. But the peacekeepers are necessary because so much of the world is aggressive, because men and women, inflamed by nationalist or racialist passions, slaughter each other with abandon. Wishing for peace doesn't create it; teaching that peace is the norm—and omitting to teach the history of the wars—doesn't bring peace any closer.

131

One reader of the politically correct history texts used in Canadian universities, Robert Martin, then of the law faculty of the University of Western Ontario, wrote in the *Globe and Mail* on November 11, 1991, that he had lost his father in action in the Falaise Gap in August 1944, and, when he read several recent texts in Canadian history, he discovered that "the Second World War has disappeared. The years between 1939 and 1945 are still there, but the war is gone. My father and thousands of other Canadians have been airbrushed out of history." Martin noted that the texts and readers offer nothing of what the war was about or what it meant to Canadians, nothing on German Nazism, Italian Fascism, or Japanese militarism. Instead, there were articles and accounts of women in the workforce or the evacuation of Japanese Canadians. "I am astounded," Martin said, "that professional historians purport to assess the social effects of a war without ever alluding to why the war was being fought." He added that he lost his father the first time at Falaise and the second time in Canadian history texts. His article provoked a flood of supportive mail and substantial outrage among veterans who believed, rightly enough, that their history was being forgotten when it was not being misrepresented again. This biased, partial, and incomplete treatment of the wars in widely used texts and readers explains much about what university graduates know and don't know.

No one should be surprised, therefore, that university graduates now teaching in the elementary and high schools emulate their professors. Perhaps this explains why a Dominion Institute survey in March 2007 found that only 41 percent of Canadians could identify Vimy Ridge as the site of a great Canadian victory in April 1917. That is bad enough, but ninety years after that battle, just 10 percent of Quebeckers knew what Vimy was, a graphic illustration of the two solitudes and the way history is taught in *la belle province.*

I suppose some learning is better than none at all. A vice-principal from Surrey, British Columbia, asked in the *Globe and Mail* on November 9, 1996, why, on Remembrance Day in her school, she should have "some veteran from the legionnaires come in and stand up there and bore us all to death with his medals." This attitude is unfortunately widespread among teachers. It should be a firing offence to be so blitheringly stupid. Fortunately, there are still teachers in British Columbia who try very hard to ensure that their students learn about Canada's military past. The war years are a part of the grade 11 social studies curriculum, military history is covered as thoroughly as is the home front, and, to cite just one example, Armstrong's Pleasant Valley Secondary School goes on a field trip to Europe each year and makes a point of visiting the battlefields. As teacher Dick Lonsdale noted, "Our V.E. Day +50 was something to behold—old men looking at projects with students, eyes brimming with tears and locating where they had been in Holland or Italy." Countless other high schools all across the country (but sadly almost none from Quebec) took students to the ninetieth anniversary of Vimy Ridge in April 2007, and one of the most moving aspects of a superbly run ceremony

133

for those on the ground or watching on TV was to see the thousands of teenagers march into the huge crowd gathered for the rededication of the refurbished monument. The entire expedition was organized by one Ontario history teacher, Dave Robinson of Port Perry High School, who somehow managed to spread his own enthusiasm to teachers across the lands. Good teachers with a sense of the past can still make a difference, whatever provincial ministries or blithering vice-principals may try to make them teach.

In most schools on Remembrance Day there is an assembly with the ritual reciting of John McCrae's "In Flanders Fields," but what is presented cannot be guaranteed to have any significance. Some schools try hard, however. At Lawrence Park Collegiate in Toronto, pictures of students from the school who were killed during the wars are shown, along with a recitation of where they served and were killed in action, and how old they were when they died. Other schools have their classes research every detail that can be unearthed about individual Great War and Second World War casualties from their town; still others put on plays focusing on an individual from the school who served. At many institutions, however, the provincial guidelines and the boards of education try to juggle Remembrance Day into relevance with the focus on a war (the Iraq or Afghan war?) students might remember more clearly than the Great War, and with the ever-present de-emphasis on Canada. Teachers at one high school in Toronto told me they had been discouraged from trying to make their November 11 ceremony "more Canadian." It never seems to

134

occur to administrators that the Lawrence Park Collegiate approach not only respects Canadian history and those who served but, simultaneously, sends a powerful anti-war message.

Somehow, despite all the obstacles, the debt owed to those who fought and died to secure our future that had been swept aside has begun to be rediscovered. As Dan Gardner, a teacher volunteer in a Toronto high school in 1995 and now a writer for the *Ottawa Citizen*, wrote, "The war is not just another subject. It is a metaphor for what Canada aspires to be . . . The Canadian struggle in the Second World War is as important to Canada as the American Revolution is to the United States. That war, more than any other event, created the modern Canada," he went on. "The war was the fight of freedom and liberal democracy against demonstrable evils. It was the just war. Canada was the little guy rising in surprising strength to defend human dignity. It is a magnificent metaphor for a splendid ideal."

So it was, so it should be. But let us be honest. When the two world wars are considered, some of this ignorance is completely understandable. It is more than nine decades since the Battle of Vimy Ridge in 1917, more than sixty years since the end of the Second World War; whole generations have grown up, raised children, and neared retirement since Hong Kong, Dieppe, the Falaise Gap, and Hiroshima and Nagasaki. The travails of the past, whatever their importance to grandparents and to historians, are inevitably less significant for a seventeen-year-old than a date on Saturday night or the bleak prospects of summertime employment.

We are almost as far from Vimy as the men who fought there were from Napoleon's defeat at Waterloo. If old men forget, as the saying goes, it is likely too much to expect the young to remember—or to want to learn.

Still, the world wars and Canada's role in them are important, too important to go untaught in the schools. In the Great War, Canada was a colony that had neither a role nor a voice in the decision to begin hostilities. All that Canada could do was to decide how it would participate. In the climate of 1914, in the even more heated atmosphere of 1917, decisions were made that shaped the domestic political context for the rest of the century— and beyond. English Canadians wanted to support Britain to the maximum extent possible, even if that required conscripting those who would not volunteer for overseas service. French-speaking Canadians, farmers, and recent immigrants did not see how Canadian national interests, *their* interests, were directly involved in a struggle between rival empires. The ensuing conscription crisis persuaded French Canadians that English Canadians owed their primary loyalty elsewhere and, moreover, that they would stop at nothing to get their way. Ballot rigging, gerrymandering, corruption—all could be and were justified by the necessity of winning the war. Quebec did not forget.

As important, the Great War made Canadians conscious that they were a nation. Half the men who served in the Canadian Expeditionary Force in the First World War were British-born. But the Canadian Corps established such a reputation for ferocity in attack that the immigrant colonials found themselves transformed into proud Canadians. Many veterans recalled attacking at Vimy Ridge in April 1917 as soldiers of the empire, but waking up the day after their great victory as Canadians, full of pride at their maple leaf badges. The war mattered to Canadians, and it gave them a sense of nationhood that has helped to define this country ever since.

In the Second World War, the depressing domestic political history of the Great War repeated itself. Canada again went to war because Britain did, though this time Canada's Parliament made its own decision on entry. Quebec was unhappy, but it went along because Prime Minister Mackenzie King had pledged that there would be no conscription for overseas service. Those promises began to be watered down as soon as the war turned against the Allies. First, in 1940, it was home-defence conscription for thirty days, then ninety days, then the duration of the war. Next it was a 1942 plebiscite asking all Canada to release the government from its no-conscription pledge to Quebec. In the autumn of 1944, home-defence conscripts were shipped overseas to provide reinforcements for the hard-pressed Canadian divisions fighting in Italy and northwest Europe. Again, Quebec's sense of betrayal was huge.

These events, whose consequences we still live with, were important, but so too was the more positive impact of the wars. The efforts of the Canadian soldiers in Sicily, Italy, France, Belgium, and the Netherlands in the Second World War were prodigious,

137

and the roles of the Royal Canadian Navy in the Battle of the Atlantic and of the Royal Canadian Air Force in the air war were impressive in achievement and numbers. Moreover, the struggles overseas largely industrialized Canada, creating factories across the land. Agricultural and mineral development was similarly spurred. At the same time, the wars brought women in their tens of thousands into the workplace, taking them away from farms, small towns, and service as parlourmaids to a different life and the possibility of earning a living wage. The emancipation of women, not to mention the right to vote, came out of war. And, above all, the idea that Canada was a small, unimportant colony could scarcely be sustained when the Canadian Corps was the premier formation on the Western front by 1918, when the First Canadian Army, the Royal Canadian Air Force, and the Royal Canadian Navy were important players in the war against the unspeakable evil of the Nazis. Canada was not a great power, but it was the most important of the middle powers, a nation deserving a place at the table when questions of war and peace were discussed.

Historian Patrick Brennan wrote recently in the *Calgary Herald*: "Few Canadians of my generation, the 'baby boomers,' or those even younger, have ever heard of Vimy Ridge, let alone its deep significance in our country's history. Sometimes," he wrote, "I meet students who have visited the now pastoral site, surrounded by meticulously kept cemeteries, on their summer explorations of Europe. They all seem moved by the experience, this surprise discovery of a powerful emotional link to their collective past." Of course,

138

the students are moved, but it ought not be a surprise. Vimy Ridge, Passchendaele, the Hundred Days, Dieppe, Hong Kong, Ortona, the Falaise Gap, the clearing of the Scheldt, the liberation of the Netherlands, the Atlantic convoy war, and the air war over Britain and Germany should be part of the collective consciousness of all Canadians, young and old, native-born and recently arrived. The wars are part of Canada's heritage, a proud part.

To remember the causes and events of the wars is to realize the evil that men can do and the enormous courage with which ordinary men and women can face unimaginable horror and overcome fear for a good cause. To remember Vimy, for example, is to recall the cold, misty Easter Monday morning, the thousands of soldiers of the four Canadian divisions fighting together for the first time, moving out of their trenches against German lines that had resisted earlier French and British attacks. So perfect were the plans, so determined and well-prepared the attackers, that the ridge was taken in a great victory. The ten thousand casualties suffered in that victory ensured that no one could feel much glory, but the pride in achievement was real. So it deserved to be. At Vimy, Brennan said, Canada—English Canada, at least—came of age under heart-rending circumstances. The great war monument there, the largest erected by any of the belligerents, expressed Canada's pride and sorrow, two of the components of the nation's collective memory.

The Flanders fields in which Canadians fought during the Great War and again in the Second World War are peaceful now, though farmers still turn up skeletons and occasional rusted shells. The

139

wars live in the memory of Europeans much more than in our newer society, and that is appropriate enough. But Canadians should not, cannot, forget their forefathers' efforts. Too much of our history was made there, too much of our blood spilled. The struggles that the Canadian Corps and the First Canadian Army went through laid the foundation for the Canada we have today. Rich, prosperous, still struggling for unity, present-day Canada was made in Flanders fields. We dare not forget. After the commemorations of D-Day and V-E Day, I know that I cannot.

CHAPTER 6

Hitler's Car and the State of Canadian History

On July 1, 1998, shortly before the first edition of this book appeared, I became the director and chief executive officer of the Canadian War Museum in Ottawa for a two-year term. This was the best job I have ever had in my life, and if only the museum had been in Toronto, where my family was, I would have stayed forever.

The CWM is part of the Canadian Museum of Civilization Corporation, a Crown corporation, and at the time had two ramshackle buildings: one had been the old Public Archives of Canada quarters on Sussex Drive, which housed its terrible museum and administrative offices; the other was called Vimy House, a rundown warehouse in west-end Ottawa, a former streetcar barn, that housed the museum's extraordinary collection of artifacts— including 13,000 pieces of war art, a large and untapped archival collection, an amazing military vehicle collection, and half a million artifacts of all kinds, even, when I arrived, 250 sealed pallet loads that had not been touched for a generation.

My job was to try to fix matters and to get a new building. For the next twenty-four months, I and others devoted to the nation's military history struggled with the politicians and bureaucracy. In November 1998, the government gave us eight hectares at Canadian Forces Base Rockcliffe near the National Aviation Museum. In March 2000, the federal government offered $58 million toward the then-estimated $80 million cost of a new building, with $7 million to come from the Canadian Museum of Civilization Corporation and $15 million to be raised from the public. We had succeeded—though in May 2001 the government announced that it had decided to move the new CWM site from Rockcliffe to LeBreton Flats, somewhat closer to downtown Ottawa, and to spend an extra $25 million to make the building more attractive. The new Canadian War Museum, built at a final cost of $134 million, opened on May 8, 2005, to rave reviews.

One milestone on this route to a government decision to support a new military history museum was the extraordinary case of Hitler's car, an artifact that caused a loud public clamour in February 2000, just before the final decision on funding. Let me explain.

In 1970, the War Museum was given a Grosser Mercedes touring car that was then thought to have belonged to Reichsmarschall Hermann Goering, the head of the Luftwaffe and Hitler's Number 2. The car had been captured at the end of the Second World War, in late April 1945, by soldiers of the United States Army, was used as a personal vehicle by a U.S. division commander, and was then shipped back to the United States. It went through various hands, was sold at auction for $2,700 in the late 1960s, and then fell into the possession of a Quebec City businessman. He gave it to the Canadian War Museum for a small tax receipt more than thirty-five years ago.

Subsequent research in the CWM determined beyond doubt that the car was one of six or seven in Adolf Hitler's personal fleet. And the presentation in the War Museum on Sussex Drive and in the new CWM shows it as Hitler's car.

That presentation in the old War Museum was dreadful. The car sat on the third floor oozing evil—but it was in a mock Bavarian village setting with fretwork hearts cut into the shutters. Dear, dear Adolf who loved dogs and children. Later additions to the display showed a mannequin in SS uniform, a large Nazi flag, and a small display on concentration camps. With the exception of the SS uniform, these were all but invisible because of the layout.

From the day I arrived, this Hitler shrine offended me. It had almost nothing to do with the Canadian Army or Canada's military history, it sent the wrong message of power about Hitler, and above all the context was nowhere present. Context is everything in history, and its absence, of course, was the problem with all of the museum's exhibits. So why not fix it? Money, of course. The non-salary budget when I arrived at the War Museum was only $800,000 a year, and while it went up to $1.5 million before I left, real renovations to the Hitler car exhibit would have cost substantial sums that I did not have.

I had been told by CWM staff that the car might be worth as

much as $20 million at auction, a real attraction to someone need-
ing to fundraise $15 million and generally strapped for funding.
So one day, showing an *Ottawa Citizen* reporter through the War
Museum, I mused that I would like to sell the wretched car.

I soon learned, if I had not known before, of the power of the
press. An *Ottawa Citizen* story became a Southam News story, a
Canadian Press story, a Reuters story, an Agence France Presse
story, and a television item here and abroad. In the space of two
days of news, the coverage of Hitler's car resulted in the museum
being flooded with hundreds and hundreds of letters, emails,
phone calls, and abusive visitors. Calls came in every two minutes,
it seemed, and I spent hours responding to every single one of the
emails and letters. I was offered a chance to bid on Joseph Stalin's
limousine and Hitler's Bechstein piano. A Toronto "heritage front"
expressed interest in purchasing the car. And I learned to my aston-
ishment that there were two more Hitler limousines, in Missis-
sippi and Las Vegas.

At least 99 percent of the public response was hostile. There were
half a dozen or so writers who parsed my surname, decided I was
Jewish, and declared me a racist who wanted to punish Germans.
I was also a tool of the Canadian Jewish Congress. "You are Jewish,
aren't you?" one writer said. "You are obviously letting your personal
feelings dictate what the Canadian public is allowed to see and not
see." There were some who argued on museological grounds with
arcane arguments about the principles of deaccessioning artifacts.
But the great majority argued along these lines:

1. Canadians had fought and died to capture this limousine and now the War Museum was getting rid of it, probably to the Americans, to neo-Nazis, or to some Saudi prince.

2. The War Museum and I personally were in the grip of "the Politically Correct school of museum management," trying to argue that the Second World War, as another writer claimed, "never happened." I was, another said, practising "historical revisionism." "We should not sanitize everything to McDonald's-like blandness." I was "rewriting history," yet another claimed, trying to airbrush everything offensive out of the past. There were hundreds of letters along those lines.

As the author of this book, *Who Killed Canadian History?*, which argued against political correctness, the sanitizing of Canadian history, the pulling of socially useful tidbits out of the past and their use as object lessons by provincial ministries of education for social engineering—I was fully aware that there was a definite irony in my being denounced for all the things I had railed against.

Even so, my initial reaction to all this was, first, that I was just plain stunned. How had my musings to one reporter started all this? Then I realized that, as a few writers to me said, the museum and its financial problems had received huge amounts of press. That was probably good and may even have helped push a dilatory government that had almost no interest in military history into a decision to fund and build a new war museum. A few letters even pronounced me a genius at public relations—if only! But the

147

calls for me to resign or be fired for raising this idea were getting very loud, and after a week, I decided on balance that it was time to douse the fires. I thus declared that the car was not for sale.

On reflection, the anti-Semitic ravers and the outright crazies aside, I have come to see that the firestorm of response was heartening. Canadians genuinely seemed to believe that their history belonged to them, and they did not want museums, bureaucrats, historians, or anyone else trying to take it away from them. Yes, they had the facts of the Hitler car wrong for the most part. The car had not been captured by Canadian soldiers, and the War Museum was not airbrushing the war out of its exhibits—far from it. But the writers and callers, by now used to seeing their past blow-dried and made inoffensive to anyone, perhaps understandably leapt to judgment.

I do not believe that those who complained wanted Canadian military history or Canadian history generally to be only the history of dead white males. Nor do I believe they wanted their history to be limited only to family recollections or locality, locality, locality or region, region, region.

This was important to me because I know *Who Killed Canadian History?* had been interpreted by some academic historians as meaning that I wanted to see only national history—political, military, foreign policy, and policy studies—taught. I don't, any more than did those who wrote to me. I want local history to be important because where we live is important: locality, province, nation, world. My concern when I wrote this little book in 1998

148

was that the national story was being eliminated and replaced with ideologically slanted and anti-national approaches to the exclusion of everything else.

Of course, much Canadian history is being published, and the subject is not dead. *Who Killed Canadian History?* was an ironic title, not literally meant, though some, of course, interpreted it that way. What *is* dying is the national history that looks at great achievements by Canadians as a whole—and at our failures, too. I believe national and local history, political and social history, must be taught and written. If all are taught, I have no problem.

As I argue on page 110 of this book—and as I also stated in the original edition—I do not want an airbrushed history of Canada with all the warts removed. A few critics of my book recognized what I had said, but they claimed that I clearly didn't really believe it. I do. Most critical reviewers simply failed even to see this paragraph, proving yet again that distinguished scholars and ordinary readers alike interpret what they read as they wish.

Let me try to be clear again: I do not believe that the teaching and writing of Canada's history needs to provoke a war between traditionalists and social historians, the former pushing the old political/military history, where cavalry charges, elections, and railroad building succeed each other in an orderly chronology, while the social historians want to include only the neglected people, especially the women and Natives. In truth, I think we all should want the cavalry charges and the camp followers, the elections and the social movements, the railway builders and the

149

workers. Certainly, I do. I actually believe in what I said in this book. I want there to be a balance in the teaching and writing of Canadian history, a balance of political and social, national and regional and local.

I know *Who Killed Canadian History?* helped to polarize the debate between social and national Canadian historians, maybe even to bring it to the public's attention for the first time. I tried consciously to do this, and I believe very strongly that this was a good thing: for the Canadian historical profession—even if many historians don't think so—and for the cause of Canadian history, which I believe to be deeply important for this nation. No past, no future is the way I have put it in the many talks I have given since *Who Killed Canadian History?* was first published.

Let me be very clear once more: I don't want to go back to the make-believe halcyon days of the 1950s and 1960s, when political history ruled. Neither do I want us to stay mired in the past quarter-century, when the social historians governed with a rod of iron. What I want, once more, is enough of a balance between political and social history that the pendulum can swing back toward the centre again.

150

I know it is very easy to generalize from one case, but the story of Hitler's car confirms for me that this is what Canadians also want. They don't want bureaucrats, ideologues, or historians telling them what to see or believe. They want their nation's history to be presented straight, unvarnished, with the good and the bad laid out. They want their children to know about their family history and their town, but also who John A. Macdonald and Pierre Trudeau were, as well as Agnes Macphail. They want them to learn about the War of 1812, Vimy Ridge, and appeasement, as well as temperance, the struggles of nurses for recognition as professionals, and family allowances. They want them to be aware of the great waves of immigration and multiculturalism, as well as the 1942 evacuation of the Japanese Canadians from the west coast. They believe that they should hear about the liberation of the Netherlands and women's liberation. And that, once more, is what I want, too.

I think Canadians also want their children to feel proud about their country. A poll taken for *Reader's Digest* in July 2005 showed that "our history" made every age group—except those eighteen to twenty-four—the most proud of Canada. The youngest group expressed most pride in Canadian sports, a dispiriting selection that unfortunately glorifies hockey louts and stoned snowboarders. Still, I have no doubt that Canadians have much about which they should be proud in our past.

What was very depressing to me was to see the anti-nationalist, if I might call it that, attitude of some Canadian historians in their response to *Who Killed Canadian History?* Granatstein actually thinks Canada and Canadian nationalism are good things, they sneered, all wrapped up in their limited identities as regionalists, disgruntled Marxists, or people who assume that all nationalism must be intolerant. A letter to the *Globe and Mail* responding to the Dominion Institute's July 1, 2001, questionnaire with its dismal results comparing Canadians' and Americans' knowledge of some

151

basic historical facts, put this case neatly: "The facts of history have much to tell us about the consequences of encouraging a people to believe that they have one mind, one memory, one soul," wrote one James Miller from Ottawa. "Selective understanding of historical fact and excessive love of nation has historically proved to be a toxic and tragic blend." To say that this wildly misinterprets the Dominion Institute's purpose is an understatement. To read into the efforts to foster Canadian nationalism today a "toxic and tragic" interpretation that implicitly equates Canada with Nazi Germany is, frankly, outrageous and silly.

Let me be try to be clear once more: I believe Canadian nationalism is natural, healthy, and necessary—and I do not believe that it is bad to have a love of country. I wear many hats—father, grandfather, baseball fan, writer, Torontonian, anti-joiner—but I am a Canadian, and that is my defining characteristic when I am abroad and at home, when I vote and when I refuse to vote. It is no sin to help children understand why this country has succeeded so well and how it has changed through overwhelmingly peaceful means—and it has. It is a terrible mistake for our schools and universities to teach that this has been and remains only a country of racists, sexists, and bloated capitalists. Yes, our country has stains on its escutcheon, and we need to study these and try to learn from them, but there is much good in our past and present, and we must teach this, too. This is a country that has fought and bled—and still fights and bleeds—to make this a better world, and to portray Canadian nationalism (and Canadian national historians) as riding with Adolf Hitler in his Grosser Mercedes is insultingly stupid.

I believe all of us—even the most hidebound of social historians—want more history to be read and watched and taught, more for Canadians to know and more for them to understand better than they have done. We all should believe that Canada is a special place and that native-born Canadians and those who come here as immigrants should know how this happened. No past, no future, in other words, and that past and future are local, regional, and national. We have many limited identities, but we are all and always Canadians, too.

The Hitler's car story suggests to me very strongly that the Canadian people want to know their history. The big black Grosser Mercedes is featured in the new Canadian War Museum, but the presentation of the exhibit is executed with much more attention to historical truth. No one who sees it will be able to conclude that the key fact about the Führer was that he loved dogs and children.

CHAPTER 7

Canadian Identity and Canadian History

In his Leader's Day address on September 24, 1997, then prime minister Jean Chrétien said, "It is unacceptable that our youth may know all about computers, but so little about their country. We must find ways for young Canadians to learn what they share, to know what we have done, and to gain pride in their nation's accomplishments. The Government of Canada will work with our government museums, other federal and provincial institutions and with voluntary groups to develop ways to increase Canadians' knowledge of what we have done together."

Jean Chrétien's government tried to live up to these words by financing and constructing a new Canadian War Museum on Ottawa's LeBreton Flats. The building, designed by Raymond Moriyama, opened on the sixtieth anniversary of V-E Day, May 8, 2005. The Chrétien government also proposed to build a political history museum in the government conference centre, Ottawa's old Union Station. This idea, denounced by small museums across the country and greeted tepidly by the social historians who set the Canadian historical agenda, died, killed by Paul Martin as soon as he took over the government's reins in late 2004. Why a political history museum was inappropriate is very difficult for me to understand. Surely anything that helped Canadians understand their democracy and the men and women who made it hum could only be a good and useful thing.

For let's be clear, Canadians know very little about their past. Every survey, every study, demonstrates this. The one historical date Canadians can identify in large numbers is D-Day—thanks to Stephen Spielberg and Tom Hanks. Why? Because as this book has demonstrated, history has not been taught much in our schools, and what history has been taught has not been national in scope. Most provinces have no compulsory Canadian history course in high school; some have only bits and pieces of the Canadian past buried in social science courses. However Canada's history is taught, we can be sure that there will be heavy emphasis on tolerance and multiculturalism. While very useful in many ways, this has led to an episodic treatment of history with bits pulled out of the past for their social utility. No chronology, an emphasis on intolerance, on racism and sexism, on the provincial, regional, and local aspects of history—important subjects, but together none of these can come close to telling the whole Canadian story.

158

This is sad, because we have a great national history, a genuinely usable past. This nation is a success story. We have no bloody revolutions, no civil wars. We fight with each other, but usually do so with civility. We share a past, even if we disagree about it, and we all operate in a common context made up of that shared past. Canadians share the same frame of reference, and we share not only a past but also a future—and we know this instinctively. The immigrants who flood into Canada from all over the globe come here because our past made us a democracy, a tolerant and civil society, and a land of opportunity. How many nations can say this? The problem is that we don't know our past or teach it well to either the native-born or the immigrant.

Canadians are not culture-bound, to use a phrase coined by Toronto lawyer and consultant William Macdonald. We are open to the world, and as a people we benefit hugely from this openness. Our artists, writers, and musicians benefit from this, too, and they obviously need much more government support to thrive. But this openness, advantageous as it is, means that our culture is international, that our artists operate in an international context. Yes, there are Canadian voices, but we all know that our most successful artists frequently end up elsewhere—in Hollywood, New York, London, or Paris. I do not believe Margaret Atwood or Alice Munro, however vibrant they may be as exponents of Canadian fiction, can protect our nationality by themselves.

And I agree with Alain Dubuc of *La Presse* when he noted in his 2001 Baldwin-Lafontaine Lecture that the elements that most accurately define the contemporary Canadian identity are the Charter of Rights and Freedoms, multiculturalism, and the Canadian social safety net. He added with some justifiable tartness that "the Charter . . . is less than 20 years old; the very idea of multiculturalism is

30 years old; the welfare state began to take shape 40 years ago" (*sic*—more accurately, sixty years ago). These new values, he went on, so quickly became sacred cows, reflecting a great insecurity. He was exactly right.

I do not believe—as many Canadians used to—that our social programs, our medicare, our supposedly kinder, gentler society make up or can protect our nationality. Such things are critical, yes, but these ideas and programs are underfunded and under attack and may not survive. I very much hope they do, but they may not. Multiculturalism cannot protect our nationality because, while it preaches tolerance, many believe, as I do, that it is more divisive than uniting. The Charter is important as a symbol, but in truth it is an Americanizing influence, sometimes putting courts above Parliament. The Conservative Party is not alone in reacting sharply to judge-made law. And medicare sometimes seems to fill such a role in Canada that it appears to be a health program with a national flag. If only it worked better.

There are additional defining features of Canada, of course. Bilingualism and biculturalism have worked in many ways (in the city of Ottawa and in the federal government, for example), but they are sometimes even more divisive than they are uniting. Peacekeeping is an idea central to Canada (we do peacekeeping, the Yanks fight wars, the saying goes)—but peacekeeping in the old "blue beret" fashion scarcely exists anymore; a more robust and dangerous "peacemaking" or "peace support operations" in failed states has become the norm. Our grandfathers used to call such conflicts wars. Moreover, with our pathetic military strength (53,000 effectives in late 2007 and obsolete military equipment such as forty-year-old Hercules transports and twenty-year-old trucks, to cite only two examples), the Canadian Forces are not capable of doing UN or coalition peace operations as extensively as they were in the past. With 2,500 troops in combat in Afghanistan, the CF could not mount another operation of any size elsewhere in the world, nor could it provide effective assistance in the event of a major natural disaster in Canada.

All these icons of our identity matter, but none is set in stone, none automatically unites us or tells us who we are. We need them all, but all are under stress.

Nor can anti-Americanism any longer serve as the touchstone of Canada's identity. Historically, Canadian anti-Americanism was a powerful imperialist and nationalist tool. We had fought the Yanks in 1775, in 1812, in 1866, and had survived. The Loyalist influence, with its powerful link to Britain and the Crown and its detestation of American republicanism and mobocracy, its jealousy of American success, its fear of U.S. power, was a very real force. In 1891 and 1911, elections on reciprocity turned on the question of closer links with the United States, and when it was the Empire vs. the Americans, reciprocity was defeated. As late as 1947–48, Prime Minister William Lyon Mackenzie King turned down a free trade agreement because of his fears of a pro-British and anti-American backlash. Now the British influence is gone and, while anti-Americanism *was* powerful—our Crown was better

161

than their president, our Parliament better than their Congress, our schools were better, our beer was better, our hockey was better—none of this is wholly true any longer. For years if you asked a Canadian what he was, the answer would be "not an American." I don't think even that is any longer an answer one would get very frequently. President George W. Bush and the Iraq War have given a huge fillip to anti-Americanism in Canada (and around the world), but Bush will be gone from power in early 2009.

To me, our anti-Americanism was almost always more for show than reality. Canadians emigrated in large numbers (my mother's two brothers went from Toronto to New York City in the 1930s, for example) to the U.S., and Americans emigrated to Canada— to the Prairies before the Great War, to Toronto, Montreal, and Vancouver during the 1960s and 1970s. Strong familial, business, and cultural links always existed. Trade and investment were increasingly with and from the U.S., and this was so well before the Free Trade Agreement of 1988. The election of 1988, I suggest, where free trade won the election for Brian Mulroney's Progressive Conservatives, was the last decisive gasp of political anti-Americanism. Never again would a government or opposition fight on anti-Americanism and win. Paul Martin tried and failed to do so in the 2005–06 election. Canadians may disagree on a policy question with Washington—the 2003 war with Iraq and the 2004 decision not to join in ballistic missile defence were perfect examples—and they may wallow momentarily in the joys of trashing their powerful neighbour and especially President Bush, but no one truly believes that we are all that different, no matter what opinion polls and pollsters tell us. The idea, popular among some academics and columnists, that Canadians are more European than North American is a pipe dream, and not even a happy one as Western European states begin to reel under the pressures of accommodating their large, unassimilable Muslim minorities. Indeed, the Canada-U.S. border as a psychological barrier disappeared in the 1988 election, and today our trade and our lawyers, students, and sick people all flow south in large numbers. When medicare doesn't work, those who can afford it—or who can persuade their province's department of health to pay the bill—head for New Haven or Boston or Rochester, Minnesota. We are more like the Americans every day—our shops, our TV, our films, our Coors Canadian beer.

What we now have that is new are élites who are down on the country—Canada is a third-world nation, they say—and who yearn for a single currency, U.S. tax rates, weaker social programs. This is very damaging. The point, I suggest, is that anti-Americanism is truly gone as a definer of our identity when increasing numbers of well-off Canadians (and former prime ministers) send their children to U.S. universities, fly off to the Mayo Clinic for their operations, and deep down want to be Yankees. I don't like this at all, but neither do I want to have mindless anti-Americanism determine our politics ever again. The Linda McQuaigs and Maude Barlows really cannot ever again be allowed to set the terms of public debate.

So what is unassailably left? What is uniquely Canadian? The attachment to land and family. Quebec *survivance*. Institutions.

163

Our deep-rooted traditions of order and civility. And our history, our belief that we have done great things together in the past and can do them again in the future.

To me, history is the key to Canadian identity—for both the native-born and immigrants. It explains why we are as we are. It is a road map that shows us where we have been, makes the present comprehensible, and points to our future. It is the reason people come from all over the world to join us—because they know we are stable and change through evolution, not revolution; that we don't kill our leaders in coups and drag their corpses through the streets; that we are tolerant, free, and democratic. Those traits have been established by our history. Moreover, Canada's history, unlike our culture, is *unique*. It is ours alone, and no other nation can have it. And although we disagree on interpretations of our past, history unites us because we argue about the same things and operate in the same context. Moreover, we all—except the élites and the left, who enjoy wallowing in our sins—know this country has been a huge success in global terms, and that Sir Wilfrid Laurier was right in 1904 when he said that the twentieth century belonged to Canada. It did, and so will the twenty-first.

164

Part of the problem is that for forty years we have been told by our historians only that Canada is a country of limited identities—which it is, very many limited identities. If you write about small subjects, you can be forgiven for thinking that that is all there is. But we all wear many hats: we are men or women, Québécois or British Columbians, fans of the Canadiens or the Canucks, Protestants or

Muslims, "ethnics" or Anglos. All those hats make us what we are; all those hats together make us Canadians. If you write about larger, national subjects, as I have done—the wars, the military, the public service, economic policy, foreign policy, and the Liberal and Conservative parties—you might be forgiven for believing there is more to Canada than limited identities. The truth, of course, is that limited identities coexist, sometimes happily, sometimes less so, within the larger national and pan-Canadian identity. The problem is that most Canadian historians have forgotten the second part of that equation—the larger national and pan-Canadian identity.

I have no doubt that the Canadian people want to know their national history as well as to discover more about their limited identities. I think this has been a growing force ever since Pierre Berton's wonderful histories of the building of the Canadian Pacific and since the fiftieth and sixtieth anniversaries of D-Day, the fiftieth and sixtieth anniversaries of V-E Day, and the April 2007 ninetieth anniversary of the taking of Vimy Ridge drew huge attention in the media. There is more: the growing crowds at each year's Remembrance Day services; the moving speech of Governor General Adrienne Clarkson at the unveiling of the Tomb of the Unknown Soldier in May 2000; and the extraordinary success of the CBC's *Canada: A People's History*, which demonstrated the public's desire to know more about Canada's history, with 2.4 million viewers on average—including a proportionate number in Quebec—watching each of the episodes. So too do the numbers in a *Maclean's* Environics poll in 1999 that found 97 percent think it is important for school-age children to learn a great deal about Canadian history, while 88 percent said that they personally were interested in learning about Canadian history.

Regretfully, I have given up on academic Canadian history as a vehicle for encouraging public interest in our past. The academics in the majority reject history as narrative—narrative the public wants. Most of them do heavily detailed, theoretically dense work that the public simply will not read. It is fine to write for the six other historians who share your specialty, but no one else will read it or pay the university-press price for a badly written book. The vast majority of academic Canadian historians seem to be anti-nationalist—which is a legitimate position—but they appear to have no interest in the nation historically—which isn't.

To me, national history—political, policy, constitutional, military, foreign policy, Canada-U.S.—matters and must be taught. Not exclusively, of course, but taught along with social, economic, labour, regional, Aboriginal, and feminist history. That idea is rejected by academic historians, while it is hailed by non-academics—ordinary folks—who see a crying need to teach the nation's history. There is a clear division between the public and the practitioners, and, giving up on the practitioners, I turn elsewhere.

When I was at the Canadian War Museum between 1998 and 2000, I made more than a hundred speeches all across the country—trying to get ordinary Canadians to press their federal government for a new War Museum, yes, but also to press their provincial governments to put more history in the elementary and high schools. There was some resulting pressure, but by and large it has not worked. The education bureaucracies within the provincial bureaucracies, it appears, can be budged only with dynamite.

I continue to hope that Historica, the still young foundation, will galvanize the forces for change. Historica emerged when Red Wilson, then of BCE, read *Who Killed Canadian History?*, made a speech about the need for Canadians to know their past, and offered $500,000 of his own money to get the foundation started. In effect, he was saying history was too important to be left to the academics, and he was right. That led the CRB Foundation to throw itself behind Wilson, to agree to match dollar for dollar up to $25 million what he could raise, and Historica was in business. Historica does history fairs and Heritage Minutes—which CRB started—but it has also moved into new areas, with teachers' summer institutes and the funding of chairs in history in a few Canadian universities. I hope it will someday help to support the publication of popular and readable history. Unfortunately, for almost a decade, Historica has been dominated by the antinational historians who control our university history departments, their acolytes in the high schools, and the theorists in faculties of education. It became a reactionary force, not a progressive one. Under new leadership since late 2006, with former diplomat Colin Robertson as its president, it now has the opportunity for a new beginning.

The Dominion Institute has had a much greater impact than Historica. It started in 1997 and is now spending almost $2 million a year running a website, operating the Memory Project, which trains veterans to go into schools to tell children about their overseas experiences, taking surveys of the public's knowledge of Canada (I know professional historians criticize, I know teachers object, but they're wrong), sponsoring the Baldwin-Lafontaine Lectures, publishing books and operating multicultural programs, and getting massive coverage in the media. The Dominion Institute has done more than any other public or private institution to encourage interest in Canadian history, and in a very short time. If it didn't exist, we would need to invent it. Its leader, Rudyard Griffiths, has a knack for fundraising, for getting publicity, and for harnessing people to get behind his ideas.

Canada's National History Society, founded out of the Hudson's Bay Company and its magazine, *The Beaver*, has also been a success. Its awards for high school history teachers have attracted substantial notice, and the Pierre Berton Award for the writing of popular Canadian history is a worthy endeavour as well. Like Historica and the Dominion Institute, Canada's National History Society is privately financed. I know this frightens some who fear there are capitalist agendas hidden under every unmade bed, but there is not a shred of evidence that these foundations' supporters have shaped how they present history. If the supporters, not the teachers, in fact, had had more influence in Historica, it might have done much more of what its originators wanted: to get Canada's national history back into the schools and the public consciousness.

Ultimately, there are limits to what foundations can do. I believe that the federal government has to become the major player in pressing Canada's history forward. In the final chapter, I will offer some suggestions.

CHAPTER 8

Resurrecting Canadian History

"Nobody wants to talk about Canada," Brian Moore has one of the characters in his early novel *The Luck of Ginger Coffey* say. "Canada is a bore." I might paraphrase this comment only slightly to say that "no one wants to talk about Canada's national history. It's a bore."

We certainly treat it that way. Yet no history that involves massive immigration across fierce seas in small boats or cramped ocean liners; that recounts wresting a half-continent from the wilderness, settling it, and constructing great cities and small towns; that includes wars at home and abroad, and the struggles for dignity and success of countless ordinary men, women, and children can be boring. But somehow, for all the reasons laid out in this book, we have all but killed Canadian history.

Who, in particular, is responsible for this decimation of our history?

173

- The provincial ministries of education for preaching and practising parochial regionalism and for gutting their curricula of content.
- The ministry bureaucrats who have pressed the "whole child" approach and anti-élitist education.
- The ethnic communities that have been conned by Canada's multiculturalism policy into demanding an offence-free education for all Canadian children, so that the idea that Canada has a past and a culture has been all but lost.
- The boards of education that have responded to pressures for political correctness by denuding their curricula of serious knowledge and offering only trendy pap.
- The media that have looked only for scandal and for a new approach to the past, so that fact becomes half-truth and feeds only cynicism.
- The university professors who have waged internecine wars to such an extent that they have virtually destroyed history, and especially Canadian history, as a serious discipline.
- The university presses and the government-financed agencies that subsidize professors for publishing unreadable books on minuscule subjects.
- The federal governments that have been afraid to reach over provincial governments and the school boards to give Canadians what they want and need: a sense that they live in a nation with a glorious past and a great future.

Our history is dead or perhaps on life support. Can it be restored to life?

The basic task falls to parents, who must tell their teachers and principals, their school trustees and school boards, and their provincial governments that they want their children to learn the history of their country. They must demand that Canadian history be set properly in the context of the West and of the world, where it belongs. They must insist that it be Canadian history, not history filtered through a provincial or a regional lens or given a multicultural tilt. By all means, Nova Scotia and Alberta should teach about their histories and their regions, but they must teach about Canada's past, too. Of course, Native history should be studied, just as that of the immigrants who made Canada what it is. But the history of the nation and the world must be learned as well. There should be a minimum of three years of compulsory history in the elementary schools, and a further three courses in high school. And these courses must be grounded solidly in chronology and must treat both the political and the social history of the nation. They must teach students how the nation and the world work, how our civilization developed, and why it values the concepts that it does.

Parents should also support every attempt to raise standards, to have their children pushed to the maximum in class. Every effort at testing literacy, every attempt to establish provincial and national standards in history and every other subject should be enthusiastically welcomed. Canadian schools at every level from kindergarten to university, despite what we tell ourselves, can and must be better. We deserve this. We pay vast sums for education, and we are simply not getting the returns we should.

The nation needs clear, measurable standards for history. The United States' effort to secure such standards failed despite the best efforts of educators, but that is no reason for Canadians not to try. Simply talking about standards would increase interest and focus attention. First, the federal government might consider establishing a Centre for Canadian History and locating it near, but not at, a major university. The centre should have the task of drawing up history standards for the elementary and high schools, testing them in selected classrooms, and commissioning the writing of textbooks for elementary and high schools that reflect these standards. Once the ground has been thoroughly prepared, the prime minister could call a conference of the Council of Ministers of Education to sell these standards to the provinces. The goal should be a common curriculum of compulsory history courses in the elementary schools and high schools—with added provincial wrinkles. Of course, Quebec nationalists will scream, British Columbia's premier will posture, and Ontario's education minister will look hurt when his own government's paltry efforts at teaching history are compared with what they could and should be. But perhaps the effort might change the way the past is presented to Canadian students. At the very least, such an effort would demonstrate that Ottawa thinks the Canadian past is important, a force for unity in a country that desperately needs to strengthen the bonds that tie it together. Our common past is one such bond.

Polling strongly suggests Canadians would support such steps. Pollara, in 2002, found that 87 percent supported a Canadian history requirement before graduation from high school. At the same time, 68 percent rejected the provinces setting the history curriculum and wanted national guidelines. There was also high interest in having national themes and events in such a Canadian history course. In other words, the feds would likely be on safe ground if they moved forward on Canadian history standards and guidelines.

The federal government could use the same meeting of ministers to announce the creation of a scheme of Canadian Scholarships, lightly modelled on the National Merit Scholarships in the United States or, even better, on the *Studienstiftung des Deutschen Volkes*. Early on in the grade 11 year, all the students who wished to participate could pay a small fee to write examinations in various subject areas, most definitely including Canadian history. These examinations would be marked by a national panel of teachers and professors. The best students, no more than five hundred each year, would receive the designation of Canadian Scholar and, say, $5,000 for each year of university in which they maintain an A average. The cash is important, but the Canadian Scholar designation, if the scheme is rigorously selective, will be worth even more at university admission time, and in prestige. For Ottawa to say that intelligence and hard work matter, that brains constitute a healthy élitism, would be a tonic for every educator—and for students who have been raised to believe that having brains defines one as a nerd.

In its Speech from the Throne and its Leader's Day address on September 23 and 24, 1997, the Chrétien government announced as a millennium project a huge endowment fund to finance university scholarships for low- and middle-income students. Merit, not just economic status, is part of the assessment for the Millennium Scholarships' Excellence Awards. The inclusion of academic results in such a program in a country that ordinarily fails to reward merit is a major step forward for which the government deserves plaudits.

There is much more to be done. Ottawa could announce its intention to use this Centre for Canadian History to direct a scheme to feed the best students in our high schools a richer diet than they now receive. Every high school that wishes to do so could teach its best students history (and, if we are wise, literature, mathematics, and science) at a first-year university level, and have those students sit a national test in each of the subjects studied. In history, such tests must contain a substantial piece of writing, and the examinations again should be centrally marked. Such courses should ordinarily be taught in the last year of high school, and the grades could be given on the normal A-to-F system. The universities should be pushed and cajoled into giving two single-semester credits to a student with an A grade. A first-rate student, sitting three or four tests, could enter university with most of the first year already done, and this plan would permit either an accelerated university degree or extra flexibility in taking or delaying courses. Above all, such a scheme would again encourage the best students and the best high school teachers. The costs might be substantial, but Ottawa could carry them as a useful federal intrusion into the educational field.

Ottawa could also take other useful measures, such as offering elementary schools, high schools, community colleges, and public libraries grants to purchase books in Canadian history. Every library in Canada has seen its budgets cut in the last decade or more and has purchased few new books. The federal government could undertake a five-year program to give each library one hundred books a year about Canadian history. I estimate there are at least five thousand libraries in Canada, which would mean five thousand copies of each book. The books should be purchased from publishers—who would have to reprint and put many titles back on sale. This would be good for publishers, most of whom are on the brink of collapse because of the returns policy and predatory pricing of the country's one large bookselling chain. This would give royalties to authors, 90 percent of whom usually make nothing from their work. A program such as this could be a cheap and simple way to help libraries, publishers, and authors. Moreover, why not offer these libraries subscriptions to historical journals— *The Beaver*, for example? These measures would cost relatively little and, most important, would help students and citizens learn about their country. And why not have the Canadian International Development Agency buy Canadian books for universities abroad? Why not have the Department of Foreign Affairs have good historical libraries in each embassy and consulate? These, frankly, are the only ways Canadian history will get out into the world.

The government could fund a truly first-rate Canadian history website and speed up the process of putting national archival records online. It could set up a clearinghouse, possibly located at the Centre for Canadian History, for the distribution of Canadian history materials. And it could have the Canadian Heritage ministry offer additional financial support for television and radio history programs. A first-rate television series set around Canada's national historic sites, for example, would be a natural. Two-thirds of Canadians in the *Maclean's* poll cited earlier said that if the programming was available, they would turn to TV to learn more Canadian history. So let's call their bluff: why not give them the programs?

Because I had the opportunity to spend two years at the Canadian War Museum, I learned much about museums, an area I knew nothing about before. We hired for the Canadian War Museum first-rate historians, who came because they realized a museum could reach hundreds of thousands Canadians more with their past than any lecture in a university classroom or any shelf of books. What Victor Rabinovitch, the president of the Canadian Museum of Civilization, has called "the challenge of shaping public memory" can attract first-rate scholars and first-rate minds to take on the task. The new War Museum, with more than a million visitors in its first eighteen months of operation, is doing precisely that. Museums are powerful tools the federal government can and should use to present the nation's history to the people. And national museums should tell the national story. This does not mean propaganda. Nor does it mean telling a standardized, bland consensus account.

It does mean telling the story, warts and all, though it should not mean wallowing in victimology or letting curators try to paint Canadians as genocidal monsters. I believe the Canadian story is overwhelmingly a positive one and that, if told straight and honestly, the message will get out.

If I had a free hand, I'd create three new Canadian War Museums (using the Navy's Maritime Command Museum in Halifax, the Canadian Warplane Heritage Museum in Hamilton, and the Military Museums in Calgary—the former Museum of the Regiments) to ensure that the existing small military museums based on regiments do not see their collections sold when the veterans all die off and the militia regiments wither away. I would also create a new National Museum of Immigration and Settlement and put it in Regina or Saskatoon, to tell a story of great success. I agree with federal support for the Asper family's Human Rights Museum in Winnipeg (though it will be a huge challenge to establish its storyline and to contain the fighting as each ethnic group jostles for space to demonstrate how it has suffered—and how those in the next gallery were responsible). I would keep the National Portrait Gallery in Ottawa where it belongs and finish the renovations of the old United States Embassy building, on which $9 million has already been spent, to house it in a prime location across from Parliament Hill. I would give the Portrait Gallery and every one of the national museums the money to send exhibits to museums and art galleries in every part of the nation on a continuous basis.

The federal government also could readily emulate two useful foreign innovations. For more than three decades, American foundations, businesses, and trade unions have supported local, state, and national competitions for students in primary and high schools under the rubric of National History Day. Each year, tens of thousands of children produce historical videos, interview veterans or workers, gather documents, and write essays on a broad historical topic. The results are increasingly sophisticated, the interest generated is huge, and there are prizes that inspire students and teachers to discover their local, regional, and national past. Why should we not have a similar plan here, one that brings together students in French and English from every province and territory? The costs are relatively small—my estimate is about $500,000 a year—and the benefits in student involvement and in creating an appreciation of the nation's past could be very substantial indeed. In France, moreover, on a September weekend, the government opens more than 10,000 monuments and public and private museums free of charge; schedules and coordinates thousands of events—from open houses to talks to participatory recreations— all devoted to the nation's rich past; and publishes a book-size program setting out what's on and where. This history and heritage festival is hugely successful for adults and children. Such a Canadian event could dovetail neatly with Canadian History Day, as a Canadian school program might well be called.

Yet another federal effort might be to establish five chairs in national history, one in each region, in Canadian universities. The

182

government funds multicultural history chairs, and it has established chairs in strategic studies across the country, one or two of which encompass some military history. Why should it not put up money for the study of Canada's national history, defined as political history? Some of the social historians might object, as they did to the establishment of strategic studies chairs, but so what? It is always going to be hard to move universities and departments that are proud of their autonomy. National history chairs would be an intrusion, yes, but one solidly based on precedent, and their creation might help speed the movement toward the study of national history that is already under way in universities abroad.

These ideas will cost money, small amounts from very large federal and provincial budgets. They involve difficult political and academic choices, and they would undoubtedly involve Ottawa in wordy skirmishes with the provinces. But our governments are elected to serve us, and sometimes they don't do their jobs very well. To have provincial governments that actually pushed their students to learn and to achieve in school would be a proper use of public funds. To have a national government that acted as if it actually represented the nation would be a change that is long overdue. Prime Minister Stephen Harper wants to decentralize federalism and give provinces more power. This may be a good or bad idea (I think it's terrible), but if the nation is to be held together, its psychic bonds need to be strengthened. Putting a few dollars into the ideas I have suggested to improve Canadians' understanding of their shared past might be one way to do this.

183

Canadians are the world's most fortunate of peoples. We live at a North American standard of living and yet have few of the burdens and difficulties that beset the superpower to our south. We have a past of selfless service to freedom and democracy; we are all but free of atrocities; and our national sins, weighed in the global balance, are minor. We have much to celebrate, and much in our past, present, and future to admire. Yet we beat our collective breasts, moan about our imagined historical transgressions, and haggle endlessly about the division of the spoils between federal and provincial governments. Perhaps if we studied our past, we could find the inspiration to deal with our current problems. There is nothing today comparable to the crises that faced Upper and Lower Canadians when the Americans were poised to invade in 1812; nothing to compare with the difficulties that beset the Fathers of Confederation as they tried to shape the dominion during and after the American Civil War; nothing that can compare with the great cultural splits that transfixed the nation's attention during the conscription crises of the world wars; and, happily, nothing that can compare with the economic deprivation that beset millions during the Great Depression. If only we knew our past, we might appreciate the relative simplicity of the national tensions that face us.

History is no panacea for our national ailments. But a nation cannot forget its past, obliterate it, subdivide it into micro-histories, alter it, and bury it. Too often in the past half-century, Canadians seem to have done just that, and it is time to restore the past to its proper place in our national cultural consciousness, in our schools and universities, and in our public discourse.

If Canada is to be worthy of its envied standing in the world, if it is to offer something to its own people and to humanity, it will have to forge a national spirit that can unite its increasingly diverse peoples. We cannot achieve this unanimity unless we teach our national history, celebrate our founders, renew the old and establish new symbols, and strengthen the terms of our citizenship. We will never be able to achieve it if we continue to allow the educational theorists and the timid provincial politicians to control the agenda. We have a nation to save and a future to build. How much easier it will be to accomplish these goals if Canadians in every province and region can begin from the firm foundation of our history.

My point is that Canadian history is usable, it is unique, it can help unite us because it shows from whence our values and ideals came (and, by and large, they are the same east and west, in Quebec and in English Canada), and it costs very little to support far better than has been the case. The Constitution does not bar any of the points I have suggested. So why should the nation's government not act? If it will, I believe as strongly as I can that we can create stronger bonds of understanding across the country. That must be our goal.

185

We have our history to restore. It matters less who tried to kill it than that we seize the opportunity to bring Canadian history back to life in the twenty-first century. It's a great story, a proud saga of nationhood. I believe that Canada's history can inspire us all, those born here and those who chose to join us.

Index

Aboriginal peoples, 110–112
Aid to Scholarly Publications Program, 77
anti-Americanism, 161–163
anti-Semitism, 111–112
Association for Canadian Studies, 7–8

Backhouse, Constance, 111
The Beaver, 168, 179
Bercuson, David, 75
Berger, Carl, 80
Berton, Pierre, 12, 72–73, 165
Bliss, Michael, 51–52, 75
Bothwell, Robert, 75
Brennan, Patrick, 138, 139
Brinkley, Alan, 106
Burgess, Joanne H., 8
Bush, George W., 162
Byng, General Sir Julian, 92

Canada: A People's History, 165
Canada's National History Society, 168
Canadian Broadcasting Corporation
   (CBC), xvi, xviii, 14–15, 76, 121, 165
Canadian Charter of Rights and Freedoms,
   25, 52, 75, 97, 159
Canadian Historical Association, 47, 65–66,
   74, 76
Canadian Historical Review, 73, 78
Canadian Multiculturalism Act (1987), 97
Canadian Studies, 8, 24–26
Canadian War Museum, xvi–xix, 125,
   143–148, 153, 157, 166, 180–181
Careless, J.M.S., 74
Champlain, Samuel de, x, 110–111
Charles R. Bronfman (CRB) Foundation,
   12–13, 167

Chrétien, Jean, 10, 102, 157, 178
Citizenship and Immigration Canada, 15–16
Cohen, Andrew, 12, 65
Committee for an Independent
   Canada, 6
Conrad, Margaret, 59
Constitution of Canada, 13, 16, 37, 97.
   See also Canadian Charter of Rights and
   Freedoms
Cook, Ramsay, 74
Copp, Terry, 75
Copps, Sheila, 103
Creighton, Donald, 69–70

Dominion Institute, 8–10, 37, 132–133,
   151–152, 167–168
Donner Canadian Foundation, xvi
Drache, Daniel, 74
Dryden, Ken, 10–11
Dubuc, Alain, 159–160

education. *See also* history teaching
   progressive, 14, 17, 25–26, 35, 55, 167
   provinces and, xiii–xiv, 14, 26–43, 167,
      174, 176
English, John, 75
Europe, 80, 87, 93, 100

Filmon, Gary, 34
Finkel, Alvin, 59
Finkielkraut, Alain, 61
First World War, 91, 100, 124–25, 131, 132,
   136–137
France, 182
Friesen, Jean, 34, 35
Fry, Hedy, 97

187

Gagliano, Alfonso, 103
Gardner, Dan, 135
Granatstein, J.L., 75, 87–88, 105, 143–148, 151. *See also Who Killed Canadian History?*
Griffiths, Rudyard, 9–10, 33, 168
Guidelines for Ethnocultural Equity in School Boards (1993), 107–109

Hall, Roger, 63
Hall-Dennis Report (1968), 24
Harper, Stephen, 183
Heritage Canada, 180
Heritage Minutes, 12–13
Historica Foundation, xiv, 12–13, 33, 167, 168
history, 86–87. *See also* history teaching; multiculturalism
  academic, 11–12, 55–82, 166
  deconstruction of, 4, 56–60, 65–67, 70, 79, 184–186
  feminist, 63–64, 126–128
  importance, xiv–xv, 5, 21–22
  labour, 61–63
  military, 69, 126–152, 180 (*see also* Canadian War Museum)
  national, 12, 40, 68–69, 72–78, 79–80, 158, 165, 177, 182–183
  national standards for, 14, 21,26, 43–46, 50, 175–177
  popular, 12, 72–73, 167
  purpose, 17–18, 25, 45, 90, 112
  social, 42, 57–72, 78, 149–152
  on television, 12–13, 14, 124, 180
  writing of, 6, 69–80, 179
History of the Canadian Peoples (Conrad and Finkel), 59–60, 126–129
history teaching, 23–24, 27–52, 142–148, 166, 175–177. *See also specific universities;* history, academic
  in Atlantic provinces, 13, 30–31, 68
  in British Columbia, 13, 28, 68, 133
  federal role, 15, 26, 83, 115, 174, 176–180, 182–184
  in high schools, 8, 23, 25, 33–35, 38, 132–135, 178
  in Ontario, 24–25, 29–30, 32–33, 49, 107–109, 113–115, 134–135
  on Prairies, 28–29, 34–35, 68
  in primary schools, 32, 35, 42
  in Quebec, 13, 30, 36–40, 68, 133
  texts for, 41–43, 59–60, 126–130, 132 (*see also History of the Canadian Peoples*)
  in universities, 33, 126–132, 174, 178, 182–183
History Television, 14, 124
Hodgetts, A.B., 23
Horowitz, Gad, 115
Hughes, Robert, 94
Hurtig, Mel, 6–7

identity (national), 92–96, 98, 157–169
Iino, Masako, 105
immigrants, 15–17, 40–41, 87–91, 108–109, 113–115, 158. *See also* multiculturalism
Italian Canadians, 14, 100, 101–102, 128

Japanese Canadians, x, xi, 14, 100, 103–106, 129
Johnson, William, 37
Johnston, Franz, xv

Khrushchev, Nikita, 21
King, William Lyon Mackenzie, 102, 127, 137, 161
Klein, Naomi, 98

literacy, 10–11, 41
Lonsdale, Dick, 133
A Look at Canada, 15–16

Macdonald, William, 159
MacNeil, Robert, 6
Martin, Clara Brett, 111–112
Martin, Paul, 158, 162
Martin, Robert, 111, 132
McIntosh, Linda, 34–35
McKenna, Katherine, 130–131
McKenna, Terence and Brian, 15
medicare, 159, 160, 163
Memorial University, 66
Millennium Scholarships, 178
Miller, James, 152
Moore, Brian, 173
Morton, Desmond, 75

Mulroney, Brian, 105–107, 162
multiculturalism, 16–17, 85, 90–100, 108–110, 112, 115, 159–160, 174. *See also* immigrants
museums, 157–158, 180–181. *See also individual museums*

National Center for History in the Schools (US), 21, 44
National Film Board, 102
National History Day (US), 27, 182
National History Project (1968), 23
national identity, 93–96, 98, 157–169
National Merit Scholarships (US), 27, 177
Nelles, H.V., 61n
Nemni, Monique, 38
Netherlands, 117–121
Newman, Peter C., 12, 73–74

Oberoi, Harjot, 85–87
Osborne, Ken, 109–111
Owram, Doug, 75, 79–80

peacekeeping, xv, 50, 130, 160–161
political correctness. *See* racism
Pratt, David, 47

Quebec, 13, 16, 30, 36–40, 68, 133

Rabinovitch, Victor, 180
racism, xi, xiv, 14, 99–110, 112–114
Rae, Bob, 107–109, 113–114
Reitz, Jeffrey, 99
Remembrance Day, xvi, 9, 124, 133–134, 164
Resource Guide for Antiracist and Ethnocultural Equity Education (1992), 108
Riel, Louis, x, xii, 4, 12
Robertson, Colin, 167
Robinson, Dave, 134
Rorty, Richard, 94–95
Ross, George, 22
Roy, Patricia, 105
Royal Commission on Learning (Ontario), 22

Sarkozy, Nicolas, 95
Saturday Night, 78, 105
Saunders, Richard, 74
Schlesinger, Arthur, 93–94, 95

Second World War, 14–15, 101–106, 119–125, 127–130, 133–135, 137–138
Se souvenir et devenir (1996), 39
Simpson, Jeffrey, 65
Social Sciences and Humanities Research Council (SSHRC), 77
Spicer, Keith, 7
Stowe, Emily Jennings, x
Strong-Boag, Veronica, 59
Studienstiftung des Deutschen Volkes, 27, 177
surveys, opinion, 6–10, 7, 37, 44, 96, 150, 165–166, 177, 180

Takamura, Hiroko, 105
Task Force on National Unity, 7
television, 12–13, 14, 124, 180. *See also* Canadian Broadcasting Corporation
Toronto Board of Education, 90, 114
Trueman, John, 113

Ukrainian Canadians, 100–101
The Unfinished Canadian (Cohen), 65
United States, 21, 27, 43–44, 92–96, 163, 175, 180. *See also* anti-Americanism
University of Alberta, xiii, 68
University of British Columbia, 85–87
University of Calgary, 68, 69, 126
University of New Brunswick, 69
University of Toronto, 67, 86
University of Western Ontario, 69

The Valour and the Horror, 14–15
veterans, 15, 119, 121–122, 132, 168

What Culture? What Heritage? (Hodgetts), 23, 24
Whitaker, Reg, 86–87
Who Killed Canadian History? (Granatstein), 148–150, 151, 167
Wilfrid Laurier University, 69
Wilson, Red, xiv, 167
The Writing of Canadian History (Berger), 80

York University, 8, 61n, 67, 87

J. L. GRANATSTEIN is the author of over 60 books, including the bestsellers *Who Killed the Canadian Military?* and *Whose War Is It?*, along with *Yankee Go Home?*, *Victory 1945* and *The Generals*, which won the J. W. Dafoe Prize and the UBC Medal for Canadian Biography. A distinguished research professor of history emeritus at York University, he was a member of the RMC Board of Governors and is chair of the Advisory Council of the Canadian Defence and Foreign Affairs Institute. He lives in Toronto.